All The Best

Programs

for Kids

A year of Sketches, Plays, and Music for All Ages

Compiled and Edited by
Debbie Salter Goodwin

Questions? Please write or call:
    Lillenas Publishing Company
    Drama Resources
    P.O. Box 419527
    Kansas City, MO 64141
    Phone: 816-931-1900 ● Fax: 816-753-4071
    E-mail: drama@lillenas.com

Cover art by Keith Alexander

Contents

Introduction

I remember working with a group of children who were to present one of Jesus' parables in the worship service. They knew where to stand, what to say, and when to say it. They were ready with their costumes and props. We had just finished our last rehearsal before our big moment. I stood in front of an eager group of elementary actors to drive home one last point. I explained that they would have everyone's attention during their presentation. It was very possible that no one would remember anything else during the service as well as they would remember their presentation. I asked them if they were willing to do something special with this attention. I asked them if they were willing to *be* the Bible for this service. It was no longer something to perform. It was something to be. Their focus changed. They gave it their best, *all their best*. When the service was over, the people were talking about the message, not our program.

That's why we offer you this volume of sketches, plays, and music for kids of all ages; so that you can use it to share your best with audiences that need to be reminded of God's best.

All the Best to you,
Debbie Salter Goodwin
Chehalis, Washington
July 2000

1
Kids and Programs

Children love special days and celebrations. They love to put on a disguise and pretend to be someone else. They have a perspective and an excitement to share through their imagination and simple innocence. People will listen to children in a program when they won't listen to anything else that happens during a service.

That's why it is important to make careful decisions about the way we plan to use children in special programs. From choosing material, to planning rehearsals, to sharing the result with others, we need to keep the children's needs a priority. This resource makes children and the message they can share its guiding heartbeat.

All You Need

Everything you need to involve children in celebrating special days or sharing Bible lessons is all here.

- Creative, kid-tested scripts.
- Suggested props or costumes where appropriate.
- A graded approach to each script.
- Helpful hints about performance options, rehearsal ideas, or anything else that will help make your presentation successful.
- Specially selected music for each sketch to help emphasize the message with printed music for teaching it to children.
- A split-channel CD is also available.
- An appendix with other optional program ideas created from a mix-and-match version of sketches and music and helpful indexes.

The compilation divides material into five categories:

Welcomes and Closings

These are short, creative pieces that welcome your audience and give a full-length program that finishing touch.

Kids and Worship

This section includes calls to worship appropriate for the adult or children's worship service. Some have special emphases such as Christmas or missions. These pieces are a good place to start to teach children how to be worship leaders.

Kids and Bible Lessons

There's a creation parade for young children, a fun rap about Jonah, and a story told with noisemakers. Each is a wonderful addition to children's or adult worship. Put several together with music for a full-length program.

Kids and Special Days

Scan the seasonal pieces to celebrate special days from Valentine's Day to Christmas. There's even something for Promotion Day. Many could find a place on a banquet program or other nonworship occasion. There's even enough to put together your own full-length Easter or Christmas presentation.

Kids and Music

Here's where you will find printed words and music as well as ways to teach and rehearse music with kids. The available CD is a split-track recording to provide just what you need to rehearse and perform. Call 1-800-877-0700 to order.

Graded Material

While many of the pieces are appropriate for all ages, some are especially suited for a specific age-grouping. To help you make appropriate decisions, this resource divides children into three groups in this way:

1. Young Children—ages 3 through kindergarten
2. Early Elementary—first through third grade
3. Late Elementary—fourth through sixth grades

Making the Right Combination

Combining music, drama, children, and performance can be a real challenge. It takes sequencing the material within a good rehearsal plan. Keep these principles in mind as you prepare for a public presentation:

1. Choose material that children will enjoy rehearsing.
2. Make sure that the material gives children a chance to share God's Word from their perspective.
3. Plan rehearsals with the children's attention needs in mind. Keep them short, focused, and fun. Make sure everyone has something to do every moment during a rehearsal.
4. Ask children frequently to state the purpose for the presentation in their own words. Make sure you continue to focus on what *they* want to share.
5. Always place a child's needs over a presentation. Use rehearsal times to identify needs that could get in the way of working together.
6. Enlist plenty of help. Give helpers a name and a role: Acting Coach, Memory Coach, Props Coach, Costume Coach, and so forth. Use name tags or hats to identify them.
7. Use children's ideas as much as possible. It makes the presentation more theirs than yours.
8. Sequence the introduction of new material. In a program that uses props, costumes, microphones, scenery, and lights, schedule when you will introduce each new part. Remember that each time you introduce something new, it will affect focus. The more new, the more obvious its effect.

A Helpful Checklist

- Select a presentation or an occasion. Identify your purpose as it applies to the children and as it applies to the audience.
- Decide how many rehearsals you will need to prepare the presentation. Plot them on a calendar, making sure that the last one includes the use of the presentation stage, microphones, and all other costume and prop pieces.
- Decide when you will practice and where. Clear the dates with appropriate person(s).
- Recruit helpers. Recruit first. Ask for volunteers second.
- For full-length programs, plan a parent meeting to announce rehearsal dates and policies.

Rehearsing with Young Children

- Make practices short and sweet. Find ways to repeat the song or piece often. Repetition over an extended period is more valuable than many repetitions in a short period.

- Use as little structure as possible. Young children are unpredictable. They will rewrite everything!
- Let them tell the story their own way. It will always come out right if they understand it.
- Try abbreviated costumes. Vary using a sash or headpiece or shoulder piece. But remember, if they can take it off, they will!
- Use headpieces held in place with sweatbands and ponytail elastics. It will save time.
- Don't pressure kids to perform. There will always be a next time.
- Expect the unexpected. Enlist a couple of extra moms or teens for the just-in-case possibilities.
- Focus on the children, not the program. Make sure each child has a positive experience.

Rehearsing with Elementary Children

Since you will spend more time with children in rehearsal than you will in performance, make it your best time. Understand that children can learn a lot of rich truths while having fun. Plan rehearsals to incorporate the following:

Develop an accepting and affirming atmosphere.

Creativity thrives in an accepting atmosphere. It dies with put-downs. Make it one of your most important goals to teach children how to affirm each other. It will draw out the best from all of them. Model this behavior by making it your goal to affirm as many children as possible during every rehearsal. Ask the children to identify the good moments in the rehearsal. Practice sharing good words with each other.

Use sensory imagination to get into the "scene."

Instead of starting with "pretend," start with something real. Think of an open-ended question that relates to the situation of the play. For example: Have you ever burned yourself by standing too close to a fire? Talk about the feelings and smells and sounds. Then, set the scene for Shadrach, Meshach, and Abednego.

Always start with group pantomime.

Get the children moving and creating from the beginning. It not only channels energy that they will use in some way but helps you see what the acting potential is within your group. Choose a related action from the sketch or play and involve the group in pantomime. For "Noah's Roll Call" ask everyone to choose an animal to represent by action only. Take time to guess each other's animal. Find a way to compliment as many ideas as possible, especially the more reserved participants. Then, change the pantomime in a way that asks each individual to "create" something new. How did the animals perceive Noah's instruction or the ark? Were they excited, scared, reluctant, curious? Spotlight a few volunteers. This is a better way to identify acting ability than reading a part. Besides, when the whole group does something together, it gets them ready for what the *whole* group will present. See "Warm-up Exercises" in the Appendix for other ideas.

End every rehearsal by talking about the presentation's message or purpose.

Don't assume that because children know the story or have heard the scripture, they are getting the message. Ask them to say it in their own words. Talk about how to live it during the week. Talk about what you are learning too.

 ## A Sound Issue

After you spend time rehearsing your special presentation, you want to make sure that an audience can hear it. Whenever possible, teach children to speak loudly enough to be heard without using sound equipment. When you decide that you need microphones, meet with a sound technician early to make specific plans for your presentation. Here are some things to keep in mind:

1. If you are using standing microphones, plan placement of microphones before your first rehearsal. Either use a microphone stand or some other place holder to draw attention to where microphones will be. It will also help you plan how each child will move toward a microphone to speak.

2. If using wireless, lapel microphones, practice with them in full costume to decide the best placement. It also helps young actors be aware of the distracting rustles certain movements make.

3. Ask a sound technician to demonstrate the correct use of the microphones you will use in your performance.

4. When using handheld or standing microphones, teach young actors to speak *through* the microphone, not just *to* it.

5. Always practice with microphones in at least one rehearsal *before* the day of performance. It's one of those *new* things that can throw young actors if added the day of performance.

Time to Begin

Enjoy the journey of taking children from the page to the stage. Make it a journey of the heart as well as the head. Give it *all your best,* and everyone will applaud the result for all the right reasons.

2

Welcomes and Closings

Rather than asking an adult to give the welcome or closing, why not use children? Here are some examples of welcomes and closings for various age-groups. Use them to introduce varied music-drama presentations. Let young children introduce or close an older children's presentation. Let older children introduce a young child's segment. However you use them, give the children an awareness of their role in getting everyone ready to hear a message from God.

 ## Welcome
by Christine E. Scott

Uses: Any occasion
Cast: 2 young children
      Child 1
      Child 2
Props: A banner with the word WELCOME printed on it and rolled up as a scroll.

(Two young children enter, carrying the rolled-up banner.)

Child 1: We may be very little
      But here's what we can do.

Child 2: We have a special message—
      This great big word for you!

(Children unroll the scroll, stand for a count of three, and exit.)

Optional Presentation Idea

Consider using the older children to say the lines, and use the youngest children to unroll the scroll.

Welcome Too
by Martha Bolton

Uses: Any children's presentation where parents might come with video cameras
Cast: Any age and grouping of children you want
Props: Video camera

(Group walks to center stage or steps out of larger group. They may either say the lines together or assign lines to individual children.)

    We want to welcome
    Each one of you *(pointing to audience),*
    (small pause for effect)
    And all your video
    Cameras too. *(One child pulls a video camera out of its hiding place and pretends to video the video-ers.)*

Extra! Extra!
by Amy Spence

For: Any special children's presentation
Cast: Any number of early and/or late elementary children
Props: Newspaper carrier's bag filled with rolled newspapers for each.

(All enter from the back and come up the aisle, shouting "Extra, extra," "Get your news here," etc. Identify one to come to the microphone to speak the lines while the others continue pantomiming throwing papers.)

Carrier: Extra! Extra!
Read all about it!
There's a special program tonight,
So how about it?
Stay for the singing;
Stay for the show;
Stay for MY lines;
Please don't go!
Extra! Extra!
Read all about it!
There's a program tonight,
So how about it?

(All exit.)

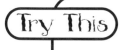 **Try This** Roll the printed program into a scroll and have all the children pass them out like newspapers during this welcome.

A Christmas Welcome
by Brenda Wood

Uses: To introduce a Christmas presentation
Cast: 10 early and/or late elementary children
Props: 5 large red hearts cut in half
A large red heart with a picture of Jesus on it

(Children stand in a vertical line two by two, each holding half of a heart. They say their lines and separate to go to the back of the line.)

SPEAKER 1: Welcome to our program.

SPEAKER 2: May God open up your heart.

(They separate at the heart and go to the back of the line.)

SPEAKER 3: To the meaning of the season

SPEAKER 4: And the meaning of each part.

(They separate at the heart and go to the back of the line.)

SPEAKER 5: As we honor Jesus' birthday,

SPEAKER 6: May you see God's love shine through.

(They separate at the heart and go to the back of the line.)

SPEAKER 7: May the reason for the season

SPEAKER 8: Become real to each of you.

(They separate at the heart and go to the back of the line.)

SPEAKER 9: And when our program's ended

SPEAKER 10: And we go our separate ways,

(They separate at the heart and go to the end of the line.)

SPEAKERS 1 & 2 *(now holding a whole heart with a picture of Jesus on it)*

ALL *(making a horizontal line, all holding their hearts):*
May you take our Jesus with you
And have the happiest holidays.

(All bow and exit.)

Another Idea Do you have some children who want to be in the program but don't want to say anything? Instead of giving lines to each couple, make one the speaker and the other in charge of props. Ask everyone to join in at the last.

Good Night
by Christine E. Scott

Uses: To close a children's presentation
Cast: 5 children who say one line each or a group of any size speaking together

(Children enter and stand in a line.)

CHILD 1: The time has come to say,

CHILD 2: *Good night.

CHILD 3: We're happy you could come.

CHILD 4: And last of all we wish for you

CHILD 5: God's blessing—everyone.

(All bow and exit.)

_____

*Or Good-bye.

3

Kids and Worship

Worship is focusing on God in order to express your love to Him silently or out loud. How do children worship God? Mostly out loud, with enthusiasm, action, movement, and expression. They do not sit still and meditate. They need involvement. The following pieces invite children to worship God first and lead others second. Do not reverse this order. Just because children are *involved* in a worship service doesn't mean they worship. If you only try to *involve* children, you run the risk of *using* them instead of *teaching* children. To make worship and worship leading the focus of your children's involvement in any service, consider these suggestions:

Developing Worship Leaders

1. Ask the children to tell you what it means to worship. Use the definition above or write your own with the children.
2. Talk about how meaningful it is to experience worship with others.
3. Ask them to explain how to lead worship. Remind them they can only lead others to do what they already are doing.
4. Explain the opportunity for leading worship that the children will have with one of these pieces.
5. Let the children discover the main point of the presentation after a first reading. Let them tell you how they think it could be used to lead people to worship.
6. Practice the piece while emphasizing the things that will maintain a worship focus.

Calls to Worship

Shout for Joy
An energetic call to worship
by Debbie Salter Goodwin

Theme: God's greatness, praise
Scripture: Psalm 20:5-8
Uses: A call to worship for a regular service or Children's Day or Promotion Day
Music: Follow with congregational singing or a special presentation of "Clap Your Hands."
Cast: Any group of elementary children who can memorize or read lines and say them with enthusiasm
Props: Optional pennants and streamers

BOYS: We will

ALL: SHOUT FOR JOY! *(With lots of enthusiasm)*

BOYS: When God's way wins.

GIRLS: We will lift up banners and signs to celebrate. *(Waving pennants and/or streamers with a lot of excitement)*

15

BOYS: For the Lord saves.

GIRLS: He sends answers straight from heaven.

BOYS: He sends answers with the power of a right-hand punch. *(Making the motion)*

GIRLS: Some trust in fast cars and motorcycles,

BOYS: But we trust in the name of the Lord our God.

ALL: And that's something to SHOUT about.

(Everybody jumps up and down and shouts for joy!)

Enter His Gates
A fill-in-the-blank guide inviting children to compose a call to worship
by Debbie Salter Goodwin

Theme: Call to worship, praise, thanksgiving

Scripture: Psalm 100:4

Uses: A good exercise for a children's class to prepare an original call for children's or adult worship

Music: Use "Bless the Lord" after the line: *"Enter His gates with singing."*

Cast: 4 speakers and as many other elementary children as desired

Props: Optional gates painted on 2 large pieces of corrugated cardboard for a couple of children to hold and open for speakers to walk through will add interest

(Participants gather onstage in two groups. Select two to four individuals to hold the two gates for speakers to walk through. Position the microphone so that the speaker can say the line and then enter the gate to join the rest of the group.)

ALL: Enter His gates with thanksgiving!

SPEAKER 1 *(after saying each line, the speaker walks through the gates to join the rest of the group):*
    Thank You, God, for _____.

SPEAKER 2: Thank You, God, for _____.

SPEAKER 3: Thank You, God, for

_____.

SPEAKER 4: Thank You, God, for

_____.

SPEAKER 5: Thank You, God, for

_____.

ALL: Enter His gates with praise!

SPEAKER 1 *(speakers deliver their lines enthusiastically from inside the gates):*

SPEAKER 2: You are _____.

SPEAKER 3: You are _____.

SPEAKER 4: You are _____.

SPEAKER 5: You are _____.

ALL: Enter His gates with singing!

(Choose one of the music options for the children to sing, such as "Clap Your Hands," or select a praise

Teaching Tip Prepare the children for this call to worship by having them fill in the blanks with their own reasons to thank and praise God. Use it as an opportunity to teach the difference between thanksgiving and praise. Thanksgiving is thanking God for something specific (help at school, Christian parents, etc.). Praise identifies who God is (all-knowing, all-powerful, etc.). Both lead us to worship.

chorus everyone is familiar with and instruct one of the SPEAKERS *to invite the congregation to "Enter His gates with singing by joining our praise song.")*

Raise Praise

A readers theatre call to worship
by Debbie Salter Goodwin

Theme: Praise
Scriptures: Psalms 139 and 103
Uses: Call to worship, thanksgiving
Music: "Bless the Lord"
Cast: 4 solo readers and a group of readers; best for late elementary
Props: Black folders for scripts

(Children take their places in a line across the stage, arranged so that each solo reader has easy access to a microphone. They carry their scripts in black folders.)

ALL: Praise God from whom all blessing flows!

READER 1: Raise your voice!

READER 2: Raise your hand!

READER 3: Raise your thoughts!

READER 4: Let everything that has life and breath . . .

ALL: RAISE PRAISE!

READER 1: Raise praise to focus on who God is.

READER 2: All His names.

READER 3: All His acts.

READER 4: All His love.

ALL: Raise praise . . .

READER 3: Before asking.

READER 2: Before telling.

READER 1: Before thanking.

READER 4: Raise praise first.

ALL: Raise praise . . .

READER 2: for God's knowledge.

READER 3: O God, You know everything about me.
You know when I sit or stand.
You know my every thought.
This knowledge is almost more than I can bear.

ALL: Praise God for His all-knowing!

READER 2: Raise praise for His presence.

READER 4: Where can I go from Your presence?
Where can I get away from what You know about me?
If I go to the ends of the earth, You are there.

If I hide behind in my thoughts, You are there.
If I experience sadness, even there You find me.

ALL: Praise God for His presence!

READER 3: Raise praise for His power.

BOYS: You forgive all my sins.

GIRLS: You heal all my diseases.

BOYS: You redeem my life.

GIRLS: You satisfy my desires.

BOYS: You defeat my enemies.

ALL: Praise God for His power!

READER 1: Raise praise!

READER 3: Raise your voice.

READER 2: And your heart.

READER 1: Sing a song.

READER 2: Make a joyful noise.

READER 3: But whatever you do . . .

ALL: Raise praise!

> (Quick Tip) Just because this piece calls for reading from a script, don't neglect practice. Children should be comfortable enough with the words and order of their lines so that they do not have to *read* their lines each time. Consider practicing for a Sunday School class or children's church before presenting in a regular worship service.

Praise the Lord
A Christmas call to worship
by Helen Kitchell Evans

Theme: Christmas, praise

Uses: Call to worship at Christmas or use to introduce a special group of Christmas music from children

Music: "Rejoice"

Cast: 10 solo speakers with as many additional elementary children as desired

Props: Black folders for scripts unless parts are memorized

(Participants stand on the platform so that solo speakers have easy access to a microphone.)

ALL: Praise the Lord, children everywhere!

SPEAKER 1: Sing of His holy birth!

ALL: Praise the Lord, children everywhere!

SPEAKER 2: Jesus has come to earth.

ALL: Praise the Lord, children everywhere!

SPEAKER 3: He gives us blessings each day,

ALL: Praise the Lord, children everywhere!

SPEAKER 4: Jesus sleeps in the sweet-smelling hay.

ALL: Praise the Lord, children everywhere!

SPEAKER 5: Sing His praises on high!

SPEAKER 6: Sing for the shepherds who watch in the fields
        As the star appears in the sky.

SPEAKER 7: Praise!

SPEAKER 8: Praise!

SPEAKER 9: Praise!

ALL: PRAISE!

SPEAKER 10: Let all voices fill the air

ALL: Praise the Lord, every child of God!
   God's love is everywhere!

Other Worship Features

The Kingdom of Children

A unique choral reading with a missionary emphasis
by Kevin Stoltz

Theme: Missions, childlikeness

Scripture: Matthew 18:3

Uses: For Children's Day, missions emphasis, or Christmas

Music: For a missions emphasis, introduce with "Jesus Loves." For Children's Day or other special worship presentation, follow with "We Are the Children."

Cast: Use late elementary children for solo speaking parts. Add as many other children in costume as desired.
   GIRLS 1, 2, 3, and 4, solo speaking parts
   BOYS 1, 2, 3, and 4, solo speaking parts
   Divide the rest of the participants into 3 groups for GROUPS 1, 2, and 3.

Costumes: If used as a missionary presentation, dress the children in international costumes.

(Solo speakers stand in front, two speakers to a microphone. The rest of the children stand in three groups behind them. Create a stage arrangement that has more curves than straight lines for visual interest.)

GIRL 1 & BOY 1: I am a child *lost* and lonely and hurting in a world of fear.

GIRLS 1 & 2: I am a child, lost and *lonely,* hurting in a world of fear.

GIRLS 2 & 3: I am a child, lost and lonely, *hurting* in a world of fear.

ALL: All children everywhere are lost.

GROUP 1: The children of China.

GROUP 2: The children of Asia.

GROUP 3: The children of South America.

GROUP 2: The children of America.

GROUP 1: The children of Russia.

GROUP 3: The children of Mexico.

GROUP 2: The children of Europe.

ALL: All the children of the earth . . .

BOY 2: . . . are lonely.

(The following is done in rounds.)

GROUP 1: We are the children in a world full of wars,

(GROUP 2 *begins*) hatred, confusion,

(GROUP 3 *begins*) violence, polluted air, polluted water, confusion, racism, peer pressure, drugs, disease, confusion, *confusion!*

GROUP 2: We are the children in a world full of wars, hatred, confusion,

(GROUP 3 *begins*) violence, polluted air, polluted water, confusion, racism, peer pressure, drugs, disease, confusion, *confusion!*

GROUP 3: We are the children in a world full of wars, hatred, confusion, violence, polluted air, polluted water, confusion, racism, peer pressure, drugs, disease, confusion, *confusion!*

(Pause; count 1, 2, 3)

GIRL 3: One small child born in Bethlehem.

GIRL 4: One small child in a confusing world.

BOY 3: This small child later said,

GROUP 1: *Unless* you become as little children,

GROUP 3: You *will not* enter the kingdom of heaven.

GROUP 2: Our faith is simple,

ALL: But our love is strong.

(Pause; count 1, 2, 3)

GROUP 1: Pray that you become as children.

GROUP 3: Pray for all children everywhere.

ALL: All children everywhere

BOY 4: Pray for you.

ALL: Amen.

Tips for Choral Reading

1. Identify a leader or "starter" for a unison piece.
2. Practice the rhythm of lines so that everyone expresses it the same way.
3. Make sure readers highlight only the parts they speak for a quick visual cue.
4. Practice with microphones if you need to use them for performance.
5. Develop a few coded signals:
   a. One finger over lips for quiet voice.
   b. A hand to ear for louder voice.
   c. Hand out in a policeman's stop signal.
   d. Draw circles in place with out-stretched fingers to speed up.
   e. Fist clenched for special emphasis.

Presentation Option

▶ Divide children into 4 groups. Assign one part to each group.
▶ Use 2 or 3 children for each child's part.
▶ Divide the leader parts among Sunday School teachers.
▶ Ask the children's pastor or senior pastor to pray the closing prayer.
▶ Ask all parents to stand and read the parts identified by "congregation."
▶ Add younger children in costume for missions presentation.

Here We Are

A responsive reading good for Children's Day
by Faye Nyce

Theme: Teaching children about God
Scriptures: Deuteronomy 6:4-9; Joel 1:3; Matthew 19:14
Uses: Children's Day, Promotion Day, or other Sunday School emphasis
Music: "We Are the Children"
Cast: 4 early or late elementary children and 1 adult

(The leader may use the pulpit microphone while children stand, two on each side of the leader.)

LEADER *(reading from a Bible):* Hear, O Israel: The LORD our God, the LORD is one. Love the LORD your God with all your heart and with all your soul and with all your strength. These commandments that I give you today are to be upon your hearts. Impress them on your children. Talk about them when you sit at home and when you walk along the road, when you lie down and when you get up. Tie them as symbols on your hands and bind them on your foreheads. Write them on the doorframes of your houses and on your gates *(Deuteronomy 6:4-9).*

CONGREGATION: It is our desire to be faithful in teaching the next generation about our loving and wise God.

CHILD 1: Here we are—with open minds eager to learn.

LEADER: Our children are our most valuable treasure. They are children of blessing and hope.

CONGREGATION: The church is people—big people and little people—all in God's care.

CHILD 2: I am important. God made me.

LEADER *(reading again from a Bible):* Joel 1:3 says, "Tell it to your children, and let your children tell it to their children, and their children to the next generation."

CONGREGATION: This is our goal—that the message of God's love will not be lost from neglect or default.

CHILD 3: Teach us the stories of the Bible. Teach us to sing the songs that you have known.

LEADER: Jesus said, "Let the little children come to me, and do not hinder them, for the kingdom of heaven belongs to such as these" (Matthew 19:14).

CONGREGATION:
We dedicate ourselves to instructing and guiding the children among us in the way of the One who loved us and gave His life for us.

CHILD 4: We want to learn from you. We are following in your footsteps.

LEADER: Will you pray with me? Our kind and loving Heavenly Father, we thank You for the blessing of children. They are Yours, but You have loaned them to us for this short time. As we teach and guide them, we plead for wisdom and patience. Give us what we need so that we will be consistent in word and deed. We aim to be good examples for their journey of life. We pray this in Jesus' name. Amen.

4

Kids and Bible Lessons

Children love stories. That's why introducing Bible stories early is so important. We intersect their interest in order to teach truth. Hearing a story is one thing, but being in a story is quite another. Kids love to don a costume and a character and get in the act. With or without scripted dialogue, children can use their basic understanding of the story and create presentations or learn a life-influencing lesson.

Enjoy the following fresh approaches to some very familiar stories. Let the children be as creative as your time allows in adding costume and props. If you share the presentation for others, make sure you emphasize the children's role as worship leaders.

♪♫ The Creation Parade ❀

For young children parading creation symbols on dowel rods
by Debbie Salter Goodwin

Theme: Creation
Scripture: Genesis 1:1—2:2
Uses: Any nonseasonal occasion, camp or other outdoor activity, introduction to the creation story
Music: "God Made Everything"
Cast: Young children and early elementary
> Select an older boy and girl to be the created man and woman at the end.
> NARRATOR

Props: The creation story is told using the symbols of creation dangling from dowel sticks. Here are the basic ones needed. You can have as many of each as you have children to carry them.
> DARK: Dowel with black strips of cloth or crepe paper
> LIGHT: Dowel with yellow strips of cloth or crepe paper
> SKY: Dowel with blue strips of cloth or crepe paper
> WATER: Dowel with cutout waves dangling in mobile fashion
> LAND: Dowel with brown strips of cloth or crepe paper
> PLANTS: Dowel with flowers and/or trees dangling in mobile fashion
> SUN: Dowel with a large sun hanging from it
> MOON: Dowel with a crescent moon hanging from it
> FISH: Dowel with fish dangling in mobile fashion
> BIRDS: Dowel with origami birds dangling from it
> ANIMALS: Dowel with different kinds of land animals dangling in mobile fashion

(Line the children up in the order that they will come onstage. Make sure you have someone to cue them when to make their entrance. To make it a real parade, consider a way to allow them to walk down a short aisle or approach the stage from the main floor. Either rehearse special positions at different places on the platform or allow them to stand in a single line across the platform.)

NARRATOR:

In the beginning, it was dark. It was very, very dark. *(Two or more children enter with* DARK *rods.)* But God did not want to leave everything in the dark, so He said, "Let there be light." *(The same number of children enters with* LIGHT *rods.)* He called the light Day. (LIGHT *holders go to one side.)* And He called the dark Night. *(The* DARK *holders go to the other side of the stage.)* And God said that this was good for the first day of creation.

Then God made another separation. He made the blue of the sky to be up high. (SKY *holders enter and hold their rods up high.)* The blue that was not part of the sky He called water, and it stayed below the sky. (WATER *holders enter to stand in front of night and day.)* It was the end of the second day of creation.

Then God divided the water. Where there was no water, He called it land. (LAND *holders enter and position themselves in between water.)* This was good, God said. Next, God told the land to grow things. And the land grew trees and flowers and grass. *(Holders enter carrying rods with flowers and trees.)* God said this was good too. It was a good way to finish the third day of creation.

On the next day of creation, God created a sign for day that was the Sun. (SUN *holder enters and stands with* LIGHT.) Then God created a sign for the night, which was the Moon. (MOON *holder enters and stands with* DARK.) It was good too. That was enough to do on the fourth day of creation.

Then God turned His attention to the water on the earth. He made fish to swim in the waters (FISH *holders enter and stand with* WATER.) He made birds to fly in the sky. (BIRD *holders enter and stand with* SKY.) That was the fifth day, and it was good too.

God must have liked the fish and birds so much that He wanted to create many other kinds of animals, more than you could imagine or count. (ANIMAL *holders enter and stand with* LAND.) That was a very busy sixth day of creation. God looked at all the animals and said they were all good.

In fact, everything was so good, God wanted to create something different from everything else He had created but more like himself than anything else. He created man. *(A boy walks out.)* He created woman. *(A girl walks out.)* He gave them the whole world to take care of. He gave them himself. The more the man and woman explored the world God had made *(the boy and girl walk around looking at the symbols of creation)*, the more they began to repeat what God had said. "This is very good." *(If possible, have the boy and girl say this line.)* God showed how much He loved us by creating such a beautiful world for us. He wants us to love Him the same way. To which we all say: "This is very good." *(Lead everyone to say this together.)*

Helpful Hint

One of the easiest ways to involve children in a story presentation is to use a narrator or storyteller. This takes the burden off the children. In fact, you can tell whole stories without a single memorized line if you use a storyteller. Simply practice cues for action and pantomime.

Rod Puppets

Any symbol or object hung from a stick or attached to a rod becomes a kind of rod puppet. They are not as complex as marionettes, which dangle by several strings. However, they can have movable parts manipulated by additional rods.

Rod puppets help you picture a story that might be difficult to act out. Consider how you would tell Ezekiel's vision of dry bones using a cardboard skeleton on a rod. The puppeteers can dress in black and manipulate their "puppet" without needing to hide their presence onstage.

(All exit to the back in a creation parade or gather to sing "God Made Everything." If using the song at the end, have children step forward to dangle their symbols high when singing about their creation symbol.)

 Noah's Roll Call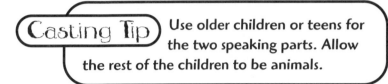

A sketch for two actors and a lot of animals
by Martha Bolton

Theme: Trusting God, obedience
Scripture: Genesis 6:9—7:5
Uses: For any nonseasonal presentation
Music: "Teach Me, Lord," "Noah"
Cast: NOAH: a 600-year-old man who had learned to trust God

> (Casting Tip) Use older children or teens for the two speaking parts. Allow the rest of the children to be animals.

> METHROPEROLOGIMONISON: This is just his nickname. His real name is much longer. We'll just call him by his last name, though—"Smith."
>
> ANIMALS: Lions, tigers, giraffes, foxes, monkeys, elephants, bears, lambs, kangaroos, rabbits, skunks, cats, horses, and mice. *(Note: This sketch may be performed with or without animal characters. If you prefer a small cast, NOAH can just pretend each animal comes on board.)*

Setting: Use a cardboard ark front that includes a door but doesn't necessarily show the whole ark. If using children to play animals, attach a string to the cutout door so that it can be closed from behind without the audience seeing anyone's hand closing it.

Props: A clipboard with papers
> Pen

Costumes: Bible era costumes for NOAH and SMITH
> Animal costumes or masks to represent various animals. Or have fun experimenting with pantomime to represent the animals.

(Sketch opens with NOAH standing at ramp of ark. He is holding the pen and clipboard with papers in his hand and is proceeding to take roll. SMITH enters.)

SMITH: Hi, Noah. What are you doing?

NOAH: Taking roll. *(Two tigers enter.)* Tigers—two. *(He marks it on his roll sheet.)* Go ahead and board. *(The two tigers walk up ramp and walk through door of ark. Two lions enter.)* Lions—two. *(NOAH marks it down.)* Go ahead and board. *(The two lions board ark. Two giraffes enter.)* Giraffes—two. *(He marks it down.)* Go ahead and board . . . and go directly to the sunroof! *(The two giraffes board the ark.)*

SMITH *(confused):* So, tell me, Noah, why are you taking roll?

NOAH: I have to make sure everyone's here.

SMITH: Oh, I get it. This is some sort of school for wildlife—an animal academy . . . a creature college! That's it, isn't it?

NOAH: A school? Don't be ridiculous—animals don't go to school!

SMITH: Yeah, I suppose you're right. I mean, who'd have the guts to give a lion detention? *(Thinks for a moment)* Well, then, if it's not a school, then it must be a club. You know, sort of like Cub Scouts . . . only with real cubs.

NOAH: Wrong again. It's not a school, and it's not a club.

SMITH: All right, what is it, then?

NOAH: It's an ark.

SMITH (*nodding*): Oh, I see. (*Thinks for a moment*) What's an ark?

NOAH: It's a boat.

SMITH: Ah, yes, yes. A boat for animals. Sort of a zoo cruise, eh?

NOAH: Something like that.

SMITH: Clever idea—but tell me, are tigers good tippers?

NOAH: Yeah, but kangaroos are better. They have more pocket change.

SMITH: Well, anyway, why would you want to take a bunch of animals on a cruise? They're not that good at shuffleboard, are they?

NOAH: God told me to take them.

SMITH: God, huh? He's the cruise director?

NOAH: You might say that. Now, if you don't mind, I really do have a lot of work to do. (*Looks down at clipboard*) Ummmm, now where was I? (*Two monkeys enter;* NOAH *looks up and sees them.*) Ah, yes. Monkeys—two. (*He marks them down.*) Go ahead and board. (*Monkeys board ark. Two foxes enter.*) Foxes—two. (*He marks them down.*) Go ahead and board. (*Foxes board ark. Two elephants enter.*) Elephants—two. (*He marks them down.*) Go ahead and— (*The two elephants try to board but don't quite make it through the door together.*) WHOA! Wait a minute! One at a time through the door, please! (*To* SMITH) The rhinoceroses tried that earlier, and it took us an hour and a half to get them unstuck! (*Two bears enter.*) Bears—two. (*He marks it.*) Go ahead and board. (*The bears board the ark.*)

SMITH: Are you taking every kind of animal there is?

NOAH: Yep. (*Two lambs enter.*) Lambs—two (*He marks them down.*) Go ahead and board. (*They board.*)

SMITH: And God told you to do this, huh?

NOAH: That's right. Now, if you don't mind. (*Two kangaroos enter.*) Kangaroos—two. (*He marks it.*) Go ahead and hop aboard. (*They board the ark.*)

SMITH: Pardon me for saying so, Noah, but don't you think it would have been a lot easier if you had just gone in alphabetical order?

NOAH: I tried that. The zebras complained. (*Two rabbits enter.*) Rabbits—two. (*He marks it.*) Go ahead and board. (*They board.*)

SMITH: Well, I still don't understand why God told you to build an ark.

NOAH: He said He's going to be sending a big flood, and every living thing will be destroyed. The only survivors will be those of us inside the ark.

SMITH (*laughs*): AND you believed Him?

NOAH: He's never lied to me yet. Now, if you don't mind, laugh someplace else. The skunks are trying to get through. (*Two skunks enter.*)

SMITH (*turns and sees them*): Skunks? You're taking *skunks*?

NOAH: I didn't have a choice. He (*points heavenward*) made up the guest list. Skunks—two. (*He marks it.*) Go ahead and board. (*They board.*)

SMITH: Well, it sounds . . or rather, smells like you're going to have a wonderful trip. (*Sarcastic*) Sure wish I could go with you.

NOAH: You know if you *really* mean that, I could talk to . . . *(points heavenward)* You Know Who.

SMITH: No, no, you go on without me. Frankly, I don't mind getting a little wet.

NOAH: Suit yourself, but I've got to get all the animals boarded. Look at those rain clouds coming. *(Two cats enter.)* Cats—two. *(He marks it.)* Go ahead and board. *(They board.)*

SMITH *(looks up):* Hey! I think I just felt a drop.

NOAH *(talks faster now; two horses enter):* Horses—two. *(He marks it.)* Go ahead and board. *(They board.)*

SMITH *(looks up again):* Wow! It's really starting to come down now! *(Shrugs shoulders)* Oh, well, I'm a good swimmer.

NOAH *(two mice enter):* And finally, mice—two. *(He marks them down.)* Go ahead and board. *(They board.)*

SMITH: You're taking rodents?

NOAH: They'll keep everyone on their toes. Well *(checks over list)*, I guess that's everybody. I'll be going now.

SMITH: Yeah, well, bon voyage.

NOAH: You sure you don't want to change your mind?

SMITH: No, I've got better things to do than float around in an ark with a bunch of animals. Go ahead and get on board. I'll shut your door for you.

NOAH: That's all right. God said He'd be taking care of that.

SMITH: Do you believe everything He says?

NOAH: It's raining, isn't it?

SMITH: Yeah, well, I'll start worrying when the water gets up to my knees. *(Looks down)* All right, so it IS up to my knees. I'll start worrying when it gets to my waist.

NOAH: Look again.

SMITH *(looks down again):* OK, so it's at my waist.

NOAH: Worried yet?

SMITH: Are you kidding? I've been in hot tubs deeper than this.

NOAH: I'm going to have to go now; I think God wants to shut the door. (NOAH *boards.)*

SMITH: God? *(Still skeptical)* Oh, yeah, sure. *(Suddenly the door mysteriously shuts by use of string)* Hey, how'd you do that?

NOAH *(reopens door just slightly, pokes his head out, and smiles):* See ya. *(Door shuts.)*

SMITH: Well, now, wait a minute, Noah. Let's don't be hasty. *(Looks up)* I mean, maybe you're right. Maybe it is going to flood. *(Looks down)* Either that or someone's dishwasher's really overflowing! So what do you say, huh, Noah? *(He pretends to swim over to the ark, and knocks on the door.)* I think I'm ready to come on board now. *(Waits a moment. There's no response, so he knocks again.)* Noah? Noah? *(Brief pause)* All right, then, if you won't let me on board, could you at least toss me a rope and let me water-ski behind you? . . . How's that sound? Huh? *(Waits a moment; again there's no response.)* Well, how 'bout a surfboard? I'm a real good surfer. I can hang ten for days.

NOAH *(opens a little porthole on the ark):* Can you hang ten for 40 days? That's how long God says it's going to rain.

SMITH: OK, so my toes will get a little tired. I'll manage.

NOAH: Look, I'm sorry. I tried to help you, but I'm afraid you're too late. I really am sorry. *(Closes porthole)*

SMITH *(looks to the right, then to the left, then looks very depressed):* Just my luck. I miss the boat, and it's the only one running!

(Transition to "Teach Me, Lord" after audience acknowledges "Noah's Roll Call.")

Helpful Hint

While it looks like Noah has a lot to memorize, try these tricks:

Watch for repetition of phrases.

Memorize the animal order. Consider writing it on the clipboard.

SPEAKER: The only way we can *miss the boat* like Mr. Smith is not to listen to and obey God. We all need a lesson in listening. We all need to ask God to teach us to do His will.

Esther

An audience participation story
by Debbie Salter Goodwin

Theme: God's faithfulness

Scripture: Esther 1—10

Uses: Any nonseasonal occasion, introduction to a Bible lesson

Music: "What a Mighty God We Serve"

Cast: Divide the audience into four or five parts. Assign each group a response to the NARRATOR's mention of the character name in the story. After you have practiced one or two times, proceed with the story. Use elementary children to lead each group, especially when presented to the congregation.

> NARRATOR: an adult
> KING XERXES: say "Ta-da-ta-da" (as if announcing a king)
> *QUEEN VASHTI: says "I'm so beautiful"
> JEWS (all): say "Hooray!"
> *ESTHER: say "Ahhhhh!" (a sigh)
> MORDECAI: say "Just doing my job!"
> HAMAN: say "Booooo!" (a sneer)

NARRATOR:

Once upon a Bible story, when God's people, the **JEWS**, had been captured by their enemies and forced to live as exiles in Persia, there was a wealthy, self-centered, and often cruelly tyrannical king known as **KING XERXES**. As most of the kings of the day, **KING XERXES** had a number of wives but only one queen. Her name was **QUEEN VASHTI**. Now **KING XERXES** gave a banquet to end all banquets. It was a 180-day extravaganza. Not to be outdone, **QUEEN VASHTI** also gave a banquet. **KING XERXES** must have been bored, for in the middle of his drunken stupor, he called for **QUEEN VASHTI** so he could parade her like a show horse. Well, **QUEEN VASHTI** said, "No!" **KING XERXES** was furious and didn't know what to do, so he consulted with his Officers of Internal Affairs, and they told him to make it a law that every woman must obey her husband. He also banished **VASHTI** from the royal court forever.

---

*Can be assigned to the same group since QUEEN VASHTI is only in the first part of the story.

But that left him with a problem. He had no queen. So, **KING XERXES** decided to sponsor a Miss Persia Beauty Pageant.

Also living in Susa, where the king spent the winter, were some **JEWS.** Among them was **MORDECAI,** and with him lived his beautiful cousin **ESTHER,** whom he had raised when her parents died. Now **ESTHER** was so beautiful that she was immediately entered into the pageant. And when Persia's own Bert Parks announced the winner, it was . . . **ESTHER!** After 12 months of beauty treatments, **ESTHER** was presented to the king. When **KING XERXES** saw **ESTHER,** he melted. Then everyone knew that **ESTHER** would become the next queen. Which she did.

So **ESTHER** left **MORDECAI** and went to live in the palace. But **MORDECAI** warned her not to reveal that she was a **JEW.**

During this time, **MORDECAI** continued his job as gatekeeper for the palace. One day, while **MORDECAI** was keeping the gate, he overheard a plot to assassinate **KING XERXES.** Immediately, **MORDECAI** reported it, and the plotters were hanged.

In the service of the king was another man, **HAMAN.** Now **HAMAN** considered himself No. 2 in command. **HAMAN** required that everyone bow to him as if he were king. And everyone did . . . that is, everyone except **MORDECAI. HAMAN** was furious at **MORDECAI** and decided to make him sorry. He got the king to agree to put to death a large group of people who were not loyal to the king or his men. You know who those people were, don't you? The **JEWS.** And believe me, they needed a few cheers right now.

When **MORDECAI** heard about this death sentence for his people, he put on sackcloth and ashes to fast. **ESTHER** heard of his behavior and sent a messenger to find out what had happened. **MORDECAI** sent her a copy of the murder warrant. **ESTHER** told her uncle that she couldn't do anything about it. But **MORDECAI** replied, "Don't think you can hide in the palace. Perhaps you have come for such a time as this."

After a three-day fast, **ESTHER** donned her most royal robe and walked through the palace to stand before **KING XERXES,** unannounced. Everyone gasped at **ESTHER's** brazen courage and watched the king's reaction. **KING XERXES,** enamored again by the beauty of **ESTHER,** raised his royal scepter, allowing her to approach.

"What do you want, my lovely queen," sighed **KING XERXES.** "Up to half my kingdom is yours."

QUEEN ESTHER replied, "I only want to ask you to dinner. And . . . bring **HAMAN.**"

The next night, **KING XERXES** and **HAMAN** arrived for dinner. Again, the king asked, "What do you want, my lovely queen? Up to half of my kingdom will I give you."

But **ESTHER** only asked that they return the next night.

In the meantime, **HAMAN** had to pass through the gate where **MORDECAI** would not bow. So **HAMAN** had a gallows built for **MORDECAI.**

That night, **KING XERXES** couldn't sleep. So he had his royal record brought in and read to him. He heard again about the assassination plot reported by **MORDECAI** and realized he had never rewarded him.

HAMAN just happened to be "sleepless in Susa" as well, so **KING XERXES** called him into the royal bedroom.

"What should I do to honor a man most faithful to me?" the king asked.

Thinking he was the man himself,

Presentation Idea Add simple costumes or props for group leaders. A crown and scepter for the **KING.** A red silk scarf as a Persian style mask to cover half the face from the nose down for **VASHTI.** A princess tiara for **ESTHER.** A black skullcap for **MORDECAI.** A black villain's cape for **HAMAN.** A sign that says "Hooray" for **JEWS.**

HAMAN suggested a parade through the city with this man on the king's royal horse.

"Good idea. Do it for **MORDECAI.**"

And that's exactly what happened. Needless to say **HAMAN** wasn't in a good mood for **ESTHER**'s dinner party. Again **KING XERXES** asked, "What can I give you, my lovely queen? Up to half of my kingdom will I give."

"Save me and my people from mass execution," cried **ESTHER**, and she fell weeping at the feet of the king.

The king was flabbergasted. "Who wants to kill you?"

"**HAMAN.**"

This was the first time that **HAMAN** wished he wasn't the No. 2 man. **KING XERXES** ordered **HAMAN** to be hanged on the gallows he built for **MORDECAI.** The king gave the **JEWS** permission to defend themselves and gave **MORDECAI** the No. 2 spot.

And this is the story of how God used a woman of simple beauty named **ESTHER** and a faithful man named **MORDECAI** to defeat an enemy named **HAMAN** and, in doing so, saved the lives of the **JEWS.**

Try Masks Instead of working with costumes and headpieces, try adding masks to your costume inventory. Use masks instead of a costume to represent animals or characters in different time periods. Use masks to allow girls or boys to take part in a narrated story or lead in an audience participation story. Attach a dowel stick to make them handheld, and a child becomes the character as soon as the mask is raised in front of his or her face. Start with a mask form available at craft stores. Let your imagination take off from there.

Three Men and a Furnace
A story with instruments and costumes
by Kathy Ide

Theme: God's protection, obedience

Scripture: Daniel 3:12-28

Uses: For any nonseasonal occasion

Music: "He's Got Everything Under Control" (verse 3), "What a Mighty God We Serve," "I Will Trust the Lord"

Cast: Late elementary children

    SHADRACH, MESHACH, ABEDNEGO: 3 followers of God, played by boys or girls

    KING NEBUCHADNEZZAR: A strong, proud king, played by an older child

    GOVERNORS: Babylonian leaders (any number) who do not stand up for God

    GUARDS: 3-6 children who tie up Shadrach, Meshach, and Abednego and die from the heat

    CITIZENS 1, 2, 3: Babylonian citizens with speaking parts

    CITIZENS: Everyone else

    NARRATOR: An older child, teen, or adult who is an expressive storyteller and can keep the action moving.

Setting: The narrator's stand is down left stage. The throne is left center on a platform, if possible, facing down right stage. The Fiery Furnace is right center stage, facing down left stage.

Props: Narrator's reading stand

    King's throne: a large chair with royal-looking cloth draped over it

    Fiery Furnace: a large cardboard box cut open on one side with strips of red and yellow cellophane attached to look like fire

A musical instrument for the KING to play. It could be a tambourine, kazoo, horn, harmonica, etc.

Rope for guards

Costumes: Everybody wears plain T-shirts, turtlenecks or sweatshirts with blue jeans or solid-colored slacks. Add symbolic costume pieces to identify special cast. Add a crown and cape for the King. Add 3 large stars each bearing the first initial for Shadrach, Meshach, and Abednego. Add colorful sashes for the governors. Add black armbands for the guards.

(NARRATOR *enters and takes place at the reading stand.*)

NARRATOR: Shadrach, Meshach, and Abednego were three men who worshiped the Lord God.

(SHADRACH, MESHACH, ABEDNEGO *enter stage right and stand.*)

NARRATOR: They were governors in Babylon. Their boss, King Nebuchadnezzar, was a very proud man.

(KING NEBUCHADNEZZAR *enters and sits on throne in a royal pose.*)

NARRATOR: The other governors always tried to make themselves look good by making other people look bad.

(GOVERNORS *enter and hover around* KING.)

NARRATOR: One day, the king had a gold statue built.

(CITIZENS *enter and arrange themselves in clusters, as if pointing to a tall, imaginary statue located in the audience.*)

NARRATOR: The statue was 9 feet wide and 90 feet tall. At the dedication, the King made an announcement.

KING *(stands):* You are all commanded to fall down and worship my statue whenever you hear any kind of music! Whoever doesn't fall down and worship will be thrown into a furnace of blazing fire!

(KING *plays musical instrument.* GOVERNORS *and* CITIZENS *fall to floor and lie on their stomachs. As* CITIZENS *begin to rise,* KING *plays music again, and they all fall to the floor again. Repeat one or two more times for humor.*)

NARRATOR: Shadrach, Meshach, and Abednego knew they could not fall down and worship the statue. It was against the commandment given them by the Lord God to worship only Him. So when they heard the music and saw everyone else fall down and worship, they remained standing. Their coworkers noticed this and saw an opportunity to make the three men look bad.

(GOVERNORS *rise and talk together, then walk up to the throne and lay down in front of the* KING.)

GOVERNOR: Oh, King Nebuchadnezzar, Shadrach, Meshach, and Abednego have disobeyed you. They do not serve your gods or worship your golden statue.

KING *(standing):* Bring Shadrach, Meshach, and Abednego to me at once!

(GOVERNORS *grab* SHADRACH, MESHACH, *and* ABEDNEGO *and drag them to the king.* GOVERNORS *lie on the floor in front of the* KING.)

KING: I hear that you are not falling down and worshiping my statue like you were told! From now on, you guys have to do what I say! Every time you hear music, you will fall and worship! Got it? If not, I'll have to throw you into the furnace! There are many gods here in Babylon, but if you get thrown into a furnace of fire, there's not one god in the world that could save you!

SHADRACH: Our God can.

MESHACH: And even if He doesn't, we still won't worship your statue.

ABEDNEGO: We serve the one true God, creator of heaven and earth.

KING: Where are my warrior guards? (GUARDS *run in.*) Tie up these three traitors and take them to the furnace!

GUARDS: Yes, sir!

(GUARDS *salute, then tie up* SHADRACH, MESHACH, *and* ABEDNEGO *by simply wrapping their wrists with ropes and securing ends quickly. Then, they yank the three men toward the furnace.*)

KING: And heat that furnace seven times hotter than usual!

(KING *follows* GUARDS, GOVERNORS, *and* CITIZENS *follow* KING.)

NARRATOR: When they got close to the furnace, the flames leaped out and burned to death the guards who were holding the three Jews . . .

(GUARDS *cry out, cover their faces with their arms, and fall down dead—preferably behind the "furnace" or somewhere else out of view of the audience.*)

NARRATOR: Shadrach, Meshach, and Abednego, but not before they were pushed into the furnace. *(They fall into the furnace.)* King Nebuchadnezzar watched the whole thing.

KING: Hey, wait a minute! I thought we threw three men into the furnace!

GOVERNOR: Yes, sir.

KING: How come I see four?

GOVERNOR: What?

KING: And I thought they were tied up tightly by my best warrior guards!

GOVERNOR: Yes, sir!

KING: Then how come all four of those guys are walking freely around in the fire?

GOVERNOR: What?

KING: They're not even sweating!

GOVERNOR: You must be seeing things. The heat is causing you to see double.

KING: I am NOT imagining this! I see a fourth person in there! But He doesn't look anything like the others. That one looks like . . . a god!

(KING *approaches furnace.*)

GOVERNOR: Wait! King Nebuchadnezzar! Don't go near there! The fire will burn you, just like it did your guards!

(KING *steps a little closer.*)

NARRATOR: The king kept walking, slowly and cautiously. He could feel the great heat before he even got close to the entrance of the furnace.

KING: Shadrach! Meshach! Abednego! Get out of there right now and come here!

(*They calmly walk out of the furnace.*)

CITIZEN 1: Hey, those guys aren't burned at all.

CITIZEN 2: Not even a little bit.

CITIZEN 3 *(sniffing):* Their hair doesn't even smell like smoke!

NARRATOR: King Nebuchadnezzar knelt before the three men and lifted his hands to the sky.

KING *(kneeling):* Blessed be the God of Shadrach, Meshach, and Abednego, who sent His angel and delivered His servants who put their trust in Him, even though it violated the king's command. They risked their lives rather than worship another god. *(Stands)* Therefore, I decree that anyone who says anything bad about the God of Shadrach, Meshach, and Abednego will have his arms and legs ripped off his body, and his house smashed to bits!

Looking for Royal Costume Material?

Check secondhand stores and garage sales for bedspreads and draperies. Make a simple king's robe by cutting a pleated curtain to fit your actor. Finish off any cut sides and hem to appropriate length. The pleats make a great standing collar. Add a gold rope braid fastener attached with Velcro on one side. Your actor will feel quite royal in it.

(GOVERNORS look at each other and gulp, then slink away into the crowd.)

NARRATOR: King Nebuchadnezzar gave Shadrach, Meshach, and Abednego huge promotions.

(The KING gives SHADRACH, MESHACH, and ABEDNEGO very large stars to indicate their promotion.)

KING: How great is the Most High God! His signs and wonders are awesome! His kingdom is everlasting from generation to generation!

ALL: Choose this day whom ye will serve, but we will serve the Lord!

(All cheer, then chant several times, first in place, then by marching around as if in a celebration parade OR end with a song such as "What a Mighty God We Serve.")

 # The Jonah Rap

A fun rap to teach about obedience
by Judy Thompson

Theme: Listening to God, obeying God
Scripture: Jonah 1—3:1
Uses: Any nonseasonal occasion
Music: "Volunteers"
Cast: Any group of kids who can memorize the words and deliver them with rhythm
Costumes: Optional idea: Let the kids create biblical costumes for the "Ninevites," a Bible-times rap group.

(Participants take their places across the platform.)

Words	Action
Remember that old Jonah dude?	*With hands on hips.*
He had a real bad attitude.	*Push one hip out and raise one hand, wagging finger in the air.*
Instead of doing God's good plan,	*Left arm out to side with palm up on the word "good." Right arm out to side, palm up on "plan."*
Old Jonah turned around and ran.	*Turn 360 "running" in place.*

Refrain
Just do it! *(Clap)* Just do it! *(Clap)*
Just do it for the Lord! *(Clap, clap)*
Just do it! *(Clap)* Just do it! *(Clap)*
Learn to obey His word! *(Clap, clap)*

In Nineveh he had to be,	*Hand on brow, peering in distance.*
But Jonah skipped on out to sea.	*Skip in place on word "skipped."*
He had no chance to hide or swim;	*Hands over face on "hide." Crawl stroke on "swim."*
A great big fish just swallowed him.	*Alligator arms in front, snapping shut.*

Repeat Refrain

He sat in darkness full of slime,	*Squat down, pulling away "slime."*
But Jonah didn't waste his time.	*Shake head and point to pretend wristwatch.*
He prayed and put away the blues.	*Palms together in praying position, then push hands away from body.*
He knew he had to preach good news.	*Shake fist twice.*

Repeat Refrain

So learn from Jonah. Start today!	*Point to temple with index finger on "learn." Stamp foot twice on "today."*
We need to listen and obey.	*Hand to ear on "listen." Clap twice on "obey."*
Just do it NOW! Don't let God wait!	*Cup hands to mouth and shout on "NOW." Hands on hips, shaking head on last phrase.*
You may wind up as fishing bait!	*Reel in an imaginary fishing rod on first phrase and then make alligator arms, snapping shut on last phrase.*

Repeat Refrain

It's a Rap Kids love raps. These rhythmic action pieces are perfect for kids with lots of energy that need to be focused. Don't be surprised if the rhythm comes natural for these kids. Let them lead it, change and adapt movement, and add some coordinated steps. It's a wonderful way to plant this story and its purpose deep in their memories.

How to Rehearse It:

1. Clap the rhythm while you speak the words.
2. Say a line, and ask the group to echo you.
3. Commit the refrain to memory first. Use it as a standard for energy and expression.
4. Memorize words and actions together.
5. Memorize without handing out printed scripts first. The kids will focus better on words, action, and rhythm.
6. Don't forget to talk about Jonah's lesson.
7. Tuck the refrain away to apply to special "teaching moments" in the future.

 Happy Hearts

A young child's version of the Beatitudes
by Debbie Salter Goodwin

Theme: Pleasing God

Scripture: Matthew 5:1-11

Uses: Any nonseasonal occasion, to introduce a Bible lesson

Music: "Jesus Loves the Little Ones"

Cast: Young children

> Adult NARRATOR

Props: Handheld happy/sad faces for each child. Make them from Styrofoam plates or corrugated pizza boards, painted white or yellow. On one side, draw a happy face. On the other side, draw a sad face. Attach a dowel stick if you want to add a handle.

Instructions: Practice the story with the children. Every time you say the word "happy," they show the *happy* face. When you say the word "sad," they show the *sad* face.

NARRATOR:

Jesus sat down on a hillside and taught a lot of people about the way to be a happy child of God. In the Bible this special part of the Sermon on the Mount was called the Beatitudes. We are calling it Happy Faces for God. My helpers want to show you what God says will make you happy *(the children show their happy faces)* or sad *(the children show their sad faces)*.

When Jesus was here on earth, He wanted people to understand how God's way made people *happy*. He didn't want anyone to be *sad*. He taught whoever would listen very special things about being *happy* for God.

Children of God are *happy* when they know they belong to God. Many people are *sad* because they do not know that God loves them.

Children of God are *happy* when they let God comfort them. People who do not know God are *sad* about the wrong things.

Children of God are *happy* when they treat their friends kindly and gently, because that's the way God treats them.

People who treat their friends unkindly are *sad,* because they do not know what real friendship with God is all about.

Children of God have *happy* hearts when they want to know more about God. People who do not want to know more about God must have very *sad* hearts.

Children of God are *happy* to help someone who has a *sad* heart.

People who do not know God think that more people ought to help them. That makes everyone *sad.*

Children of God are *happy* in their hearts because God has made them clean inside. People without God are *sad* in their hearts because they do not know God's cleanness.

Children of God are *happy* to make peace with their friends, because they are at peace with God.

People who are not at peace with God do not know how to make peace with their friends, and that makes everyone very *sad.*

God's Word in Proverbs 15:13 reminds us that a *happy* heart makes the face cheerful but a *sad* heart crushes the spirit. We want to be *happy* children of God. We want to have *happy* hearts.

(Transition to "Jesus Loves the Little Ones.")

NARRATOR *(continuing):* The best way to have a *happy* heart is to think about how much Jesus loves you.

(As the children sing "Jesus Loves the Little Ones," instruct them to hold out their happy faces to emphasize the repeated words "me-me-me" and "you-you-you.")

Gates
A mostly pantomimed parable
by Debbie Salter Goodwin

Theme: Discipleship
Scripture: Matthew 7:13-14
Uses: Introduction to a sermon about discipleship or other nonseasonal presentation
Music: "Big Things" or "Right Now"
Cast: NARRATOR
 2 children to play the WIDE GATE
 2 children to play the NARROW GATE
 At least 3 groups of 2 or more children to walk through the gates
 SPEAKER: one child in the last group who has a few lines
Props: Signs: Destruction City and Everlasting Life

(Children playing WIDE and NARROW gates enter from opposite sides of the platform to position themselves on each side. Each pair stands facing each other, holding their sign between them as a gate. Actors for the WIDE GATE carry the sign "Destruction City" and stand as far apart as their arms allow. Actors for the NARROW GATE carry the sign "Everlasting Life" and stand as close together as possible. To open, one lets go of the sign while both turn their bodies to "open" their gate. NARRATOR stands in the center between the gates. Other children wait to the side to enter the gates.)

NARRATOR: Once there were two gates. One gate is called Wide.

WIDE *(opening mouths as wide as possible with each word, speaking together):* Hello. Our name is WIDE.

NARRATOR: The other is called Narrow.

NARROW *(in gentle but not weak voices):* Hello. Our name is Narrow.

NARRATOR: Every day, all kinds of people come to these gates and choose to enter either the Wide Gate . . .

(First group enters and pantomime a discussion as if to choose between the two gates.)

WIDE 1: Won't you come through our gate?

WIDE 2: I have plenty of room for all your friends.

(WIDE 1 and 2 open their gate using the sign and their arms in a large sweeping motion.)

NARRATOR: They must choose between the Wide Gate and the Narrow Gate.

NARROW *(together):* Choose us and you won't be sorry. *(They open their gate with smaller, slower movement.)*

(The group chooses the WIDE GATE while the NARROW GATE shake their heads.)

NARRATOR: Over and over, the same thing happens. *(Another group comes to the gates.)* People come to the two gates and see everybody going through the Wide Gate, and so they follow. *(This group also chooses the WIDE GATE.)*

WIDE 1 and 2: That's right, come on in. There's plenty of room.

NARROW *(shaking their heads):* They'll be sorry.

NARRATOR: It's not a good idea to go through a gate unless you are sure you know where it will take you.

(Another group enters, trying to decide between the gates. All but one in the group choose the WIDE GATE. One chooses the NARROW GATE.)

SPEAKER *(to WIDE):* Where does your gate lead?

WIDE 1: To the big D *(pointing to the sign),* but don't let the name fool you. You can have a great time getting there!

SPEAKER *(to NARROW):* Where does your gate lead?

NARROW: To Everlasting Life.

SPEAKER: But if your gate leads to life, why do so few enter?

NARROW: Our gate is small because people can only go through one at a time. Everlasting Life begins on the other side of the gate.

NARRATOR: Every now and then a person comes to the two gates and thinks about the difference between them . . .

(SPEAKER strikes a thinking pose, looking first at one gate and then at the other.)

NARRATOR: . . . and decides to take the Narrow Gate even if no one else does.

(SPEAKER goes through NARROW GATE. NARROW congratulates SPEAKER, smiling big.)

NARRATOR: Jesus says we should all choose the same way!

The Unmerciful Servant

An audience participation story
by Jeffrey C. Smith

Theme: Forgiveness
Scripture: Matthew 18:22-35
Uses: Any nonseasonal occasion, to introduce a Bible lesson
Music: "Saints Society"
Cast: A STORYTELLER to read the following story and instruct the audience about the actions that go with certain cue words

Here are the cue words and the actions that go with them:

> OUTSTANDING: Everyone stands.
> SAT: Everyone sits.
> SHAKEN: Everyone shakes the entire body.
> HAND: A single clap.
> WAIVER: The entire group does the wave from left to right.
> SWAYED: Everyone leans left and then right.
> TURN AROUND: Everyone stands up, turns around, then sits down.

Practice the motions with their cue words. Then introduce the story this way:

STORYTELLER:

The circle of forgiveness is supposed to be a circle in continual motion. God forgives you, and you forgive others in a circle without end. As you continue to forgive, God forgives you. However, when you stop forgiving others, God stops forgiving you. Here is a Bible story to help emphasize the important circle of forgiveness.

Once there was a king. He was an OUTSTANDING king who SAT on the throne. One day he called his servant to settle accounts with him. He demanded payment, or he threatened to throw the servant and his family into jail. The servant was SHAKEN and begged for mercy:

> "I need a HAND, my funds are down,
> But surely life will TURN AROUND.
> Sir, a little kindness show—
> A WAIVER on this debt I owe?"

The OUTSTANDING king who SAT on the throne was SWAYED by the man's plea for mercy and granted him a WAIVER. But the very next day, that same servant found someone else who owed him money. He demanded payment in full or vowed to throw the debtor into prison. The poor fellow was obviously SHAKEN and begged for mercy:

> "I need a HAND, my funds are down,
> But surely things will TURN AROUND.
> Sir, a little kindness show—
> A WAIVER on this debt I owe?"

The servant was not SWAYED and denied the WAIVER. He had the prisoner thrown into jail until he could pay the debt in full.

Witnesses were SHAKEN by this TURN AROUND and went to see the OUTSTANDING king who SAT on the throne.

As expected, the king was furious that he had been SWAYED to grant the WAIVER and began to SHAKE with anger. He called for his guards to bring the worthless servant before him.

"You despicable servant! Explain this TURN AROUND to me. I was SWAYED to grant you a WAIVER of the enormous debt you owed me, and then you could not be SWAYED to help someone else who needed a HAND?"

The servant was SHAKEN and begged the OUTSTANDING king who SAT on the throne for mercy. But this time the king was not SWAYED to grant a WAIVER to the man in need of a HAND. Instead, he did a complete TURN AROUND and had the man thrown into prison until his debt could be paid in full.

(Transition to "Saints Society.")

STORYTELLER *(continuing):* God wants us to do a TURN AROUND to forgive others just like He forgives us. He wants us to be OUTSTANDING members of the "Saints Society"—children and adults who will not be SWAYED to do anything except what God wants. And the good news is that God will be there to give you a HAND.

(Sing "Saints Society.")

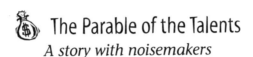 # The Parable of the Talents
A story with noisemakers
by Jeffrey C. Smith

Theme: Serving God

Scripture: Matthew 25:14-30

Uses: Any nonseasonal occasion, an introduction to a Bible lesson

Music: "Volunteers," "Big Things"

Cast: 8 children who supply the sound effects

> KING
> SERVANT 1
> SERVANT 2
> SERVANT 3
> STORYTELLER
> NOISEMAKER 1 has a kazoo to play "Hail to the Chief" or something similar to identify the king.
> NOISEMAKER 2 has a toy xylophone with a scale of 8 notes, used to identify the number of *talents* as well as the *servants*. Also plays "Do Re Mi" during the *accounting*.
> NOISEMAKER 3 has a slide whistle for *long journey*.
> NOISEMAKER 4 has a bell to ring every time the king *calls* for someone or something.
> NOISEMAKER 5 has a kazoo to play "Auld Lang Syne" when the king *departs*.
> NOISEMAKER 6 has a party whistle to play when SERVANT 3 has a *party*.
> NOISEMAKER 7 has a kazoo to play "For He's a Jolly Good Fellow" when the KING *responds* to the first two SERVANTS.
> NOISEMAKER 8 has a kazoo to play a sad dirge as in "The Funeral March" for SERVANT 3 at the end.
> 2 GUARDS

Props: 4 kazoos
> Toy xylophone with eight notes
> Slide whistle
> Bell
> Party whistle

Costumes: Costumes should be simple, if used: a crown for the king, sweatbands for the servants, and armbands with "G" for the guards.

(NOISEMAKERS stand as a chorus on one side of the stage, prepared to contribute their sound effects on

cue. The other participants simply pantomime the actions of the STORYTELLER. *Their actions should be large and exaggerated.)*

STORYTELLER *(at a podium on one side of the stage):* Once there was a *king* (NOISEMAKER 1). He was a *king* (NOISEMAKER 1) with *many talents.* (NOISEMAKER 2 *goes up the scale once.)*

One day the *king* (NOISEMAKER 1) decided to go on a *long journey* (NOISEMAKER 3). So he *called* (NOISEMAKER 4) to divide up his property. To the first servant he gave *five talents.* (NOISEMAKER 2 *plays the first 5 notes of the scale.)* To the second servant he gave *two talents.* (NOISEMAKER 2 *plays the 6th and 7th notes on the scale.)* And to the third servant he gave *one talent.* (NOISEMAKER 2 *plays only the 8th note of the scale.)* Then, the king *departed* for his journey (NOISEMAKER 5).

The *first servant* went out and began to use what the king had given him to make others happy. (NOISEMAKER 2 *plays the first 5 notes of the scale going up and down about 3 times.)* Likewise, the *second servant* went out and began to use what the king had given him to make others happy. (NOISEMAKER 2 *plays the 6th and 7th notes back and forth about 4 times.)* But the *third servant* was mad that he had only been given one note to play. So he went out and had a *party* and didn't even invite anyone (NOISEMAKER 6).

After a long time the *king* returned (NOISEMAKER 1). He *called* for his servants to give an account of his property (NOISEMAKER 4). The three servants came back with this account. *(Work out an accounting pantomime for the 3 servants, but reserve the king's response for later. During the accounting,* NOISEMAKER 2 *or someone else plays "Do-Re-Mi" on the xylophone. At the end of the song, instead of playing the very last note on the xylophone,* NOISEMAKER 6 *plays the party horn emphasizing the selfish way that* SERVANT 1 *used his talent. Repeat this part of the song if necessary to make the point.)*

To the first servant the king *responded* . . . (NOISEMAKER 7). To the second servant the king *responded* . . . (NOISEMAKER 7). But to the third servant the king said . . . (NOISEMAKER 8).

Then, the king *called* for his guards (NOISEMAKER 4). He commanded his guards to take that wicked and lazy servant and throw him into the outer darkness where there would be no happy sounds. For everyone who has and uses what he has to serve others, even more will be given to him. But from everyone who doesn't have and doesn't use what he is given to serve others, even what little he has will be taken away from him. Let he who has ears to hear . . . *(Everyone makes a noise with their instrument at the same time.)*

(All bow and exit.)

Too Much Money, Not Enough Heart
A scripture as readers theatre piece
by Debbie Salter Goodwin

Theme: Discipleship
Scripture: Mark 10:17-22
Uses: To introduce a sermon or Bible lesson
or other nonseasonal occasion
Music: "Big Things" or "Right Now"
Cast: NARRATOR
YOUNG MAN
JESUS
Props: Black folders to hold scripts

(Participants stand in speaking order.)

NARRATOR: As Jesus started on his way, a man

Bowing Out At the end of a presentation, especially the longer ones, most audiences want to encourage young actors with their applause. In return, young actors should plan how they will receive this favor. It's called a curtain call even without a curtain. The easiest way to plan it is to ask participants to stand in a line and bow at the waist simultaneously. In longer presentations with larger groups, curtain calls need to be carefully planned. Designate a lead person in the center of each row or grouping. When this person bows, everyone else does also. Don't neglect rehearsing this part even though it usually doesn't show up in a script.

ran up to him and fell on his knees before him.

YOUNG MAN: Good teacher,

NARRATOR: he asked,

YOUNG MAN: what must I do to receive eternal life?

JESUS: Why do you call me good?

NARRATOR: Jesus answered.

JESUS: No one is good—except God alone. You know the commandments: "Do not murder, do not commit adultery, do not steal, do not give false testimony, do not defraud, honor your father and mother."

YOUNG MAN: Teacher,

NARRATOR: he declared,

YOUNG MAN: all these I have kept since I was a boy.

NARRATOR: Jesus looked at him and loved him.

JESUS: One thing you lack,

NARRATOR: he said.

JESUS: Go, sell everything you have and give to the poor, and you will have treasure in heaven. Then come, follow me.

NARRATOR: At this the man's face fell. He went away sad, because he had great wealth.

(Transition to "Big Things" or "Right Now.")

ALL: What about you?

Using Scripture for the Script

The Bible is your greatest source for scripts. Many of the stories can be lifted out with little change. Identify characters, add a narrator, and use the following ideas to dramatize.

1. Readers theatre places the scripts in the hands of readers who read their parts with expression. Add simple costumes for a more interesting presentation.
2. Pantomime uses the narrator as storyteller. Participants divide into character roles and simply act out the actions suggested in the text.
3. Dramatic reenactment may use a narrator, if needed, but allows participants to speak the lines while acting the parts.
4. Creative dramatics is a method that uses the Bible text as the idea and allows participants to create their own dialogue, including contemporary treatment of context and/or language.

Consider creating your own presentations from the parables and other familiar stories of the Bible.

5

Kids and Special Days

Celebrations bring people together. They are also good occasions to have children share something special. This section takes a calendar walk and suggests pieces to fit with certain times of the year. But don't think of them just for special days. Their subjects of God's love, salvation, honoring parents are timeless. Sometimes a simple word change allows you to present the seasonal piece, nonseasonally.

Valentine's Day

God's Love Gift
Rhymed couplets for late elementary children to share
by Martha Bolton

Theme: Love
Uses: For Valentine's Day. To use nonseasonally, change the word "Valentines" in the last couplet to "anytime."
Music: "John 3:16," "Enough Love"
Cast: 5 late elementary children who will recite two lines each
Props: Box of candy
        Bouquet of flowers
        Very small dress (young child size)
        Giant restaurant bill, with dollar signs, rolled up
        5 paper hearts, each with one letter of "J-E-S-U-S"

(Each CHILD *enters with a prop for their lines in one hand and a heart with one letter of J-E-S-U-S in the other. The heart should be hidden or turned so that the audience does not see the letter. They stand in a line across the platform and approach the microphone to speak a line.)*

CHILD 1 *(enters with the box of candy in one hand and a paper heart with the letter "J" in the other):*
    Why give your sweetheart candy?
    She'll just gain a pound or two.

CHILD 2 *(enters with the bouquet of flowers and a paper heart with the letter "E"):*
    And what if she's allergic
    To your flowers? Ah . . . ah . . . choo!

CHILD 3 *(enters with the tiny dress and a heart with the letter "S"):*
    A dress is nice but tell me,
    Do you really know her size? *(Shrugs shoulders)*

CHILD 4 *(enters with the giant restaurant bill and a heart with the letter "U"):*
    And I don't know if taking
    Her to dinner's all that wise.

CHILD 5 (enters carrying the heart with an "S" on it):
   What should you give your loved ones?
   The answer we'll impart—

ALL: For Valentines, the best gift
   Is the one straight from your heart.

(All five turn their hearts around so that the name of "JESUS" is revealed. Others gather immediately to sing, if desired.)

Easter

Something New
An Easter piece for early elementary girls
by Debbie Salter Goodwin

Theme: Easter, new life in Christ
Uses: To introduce a song or message about Easter
Music: "He's Alive"
Cast: 4 young girls who can memorize lines and deliver them expressively
Props: New purse
        New shoes
Costumes: The first 3 girls are obviously dressed with new clothes for Easter.
        The 4th girl is dressed nicely but more simply.

(The three girls take places at the front of the platform, moving to a microphone as necessary.)

GIRL 1 (holding the edges of her skirt to show off her dress):
   I have a new dress for Easter. My mother let me pick it out.

GIRL 2 (pointing to her new shoes with great pride):
   I have new shoes for Easter. See, they are white patent with bows!

GIRL 3 (proudly holding out her purse):
   I have a new purse for Easter. It has pockets and a mirror!

GIRL 4 (holding nothing to show):
   I have a new life for Easter because Jesus lives!

Easter Gifts
Three boys sharing Easter truth
by Paul M. Miller

Theme: Easter
Scripture: Matthew 28:20; John 3:16
Uses: As a stand-alone sketch about Easter or as a part of a larger program with music
Music: "Jesus Is Alive and Doin' Well"
Cast: 3 late elementary boys:
        DAN, BENJI, CONNOR
        Or 3 girls: DANIELLE, BRIGETT, CONNIE
Props: A Bible

> A rough, homemade cross
> A baseball bat

(The three boys enter. Dan *carries the Bible.* Benji *carries the cross.* Connor *carries a baseball bat. They stand facing the audience, but soon turn to speak to each other.)*

Dan *(to audience):* You have all heard of the three wise men—

Benji *(interrupting):* Wait a minute! This is an *Easter* program, not a Christmas program.

Dan: Hold it. Give me time to explain myself.

Connor *(to* Benji*):* Yeah, don't be so *impetuous.*

Benji: So what?

Connor *(slowly):* Don't be so im-pet—u-ous.

Dan: What in the world does *that* mean?

Connor: It means, don't be in such a hurry to interrupt. We ought to give you time to explain yourself.

Dan: Oh, well . . . That's exactly what I thought it meant. *(To* Benji*)* So stop being so im . . im . . impet . . .

Connor *(helping):* Impetuous.

Dan *(to* Benji*):* Yeah, don't be that way.

Benji *(impatiently):* Go on . . .

Dan: Well, I want to propose that we are the three wise boys who know all about *Easter* gifts.

Connor: But the Easter story that's in the Bible doesn't talk about gifts.

Benji: Right. It's at Christmas that God gave the world His best gift—Jesus, His Son.

Dan: Right! But then at Easter, God gave us the chance to have another special gift. Listen to this . . . *(Opens a Bible and reads John 3:16, emphasizing the words in boldface)* "For God so loved the world that he gave his one and only Son, that whoever believes in him shall not perish but have **eternal life.**"

Benji *(suddenly understanding):* Sure. And He did that by giving up His Son to die on the Cross. *(Holds up the cross)*

Dan *(looking at* Connor*):* I can see why my Bible and His cross are two gifts. But what about your baseball bat?

Connor *(holds up bat):* Oh, this? Can't you figure that out?

*(*Dan *and* Benji *look at each other, then shrug their shoulders.)*

Benji *(prodding):* Come on, don't keep us in the dark.

Dan *(impatiently):* Yeah, how come the baseball bat? Come on, tell us.

Connor *(patiently):* Don't be so *impetuous* . . .

Dan and Benji *(together):* Tell us!

Connor: I'm carrying a baseball bat because it reminds me that even though Jesus died on a cross, He rose from the grave and is alive today.

Benji *(still not understanding):* But why the bat?

Connor: Because Jesus is alive, He is with me everywhere I go and in everything I do. Even when I'm playing baseball.

DAN: Baseball!

CONNOR: Yep. Easter reminds me that Jesus goes with me everywhere. *(To* DAN*)* Why don't you read Matthew 28:20?

DAN *(opening Bible and reading):* "I am with you *always.*"

CONNOR: Even when I'm playing baseball!

(All three turn to face the audience for the last three lines.)

BENJI: That's the story of Easter.

CONNOR: According to . . .

DAN: Us three wise boys.

Easter Joy

A young child's Easter presentation
by Tim Miller and Debbie Goodwin

Theme: Easter

Uses: A young children's presentation for Easter

Music: Use the following songs in order after a two-line presentation: "Hosanna" "Clap Your Hands," and "Jesus Loves the Little Ones."

Cast: 2 children to deliver a two-line piece
      Child to be Jesus
      Child to be a donkey on all fours

Props: Palm branches for each child
      A large corrugated cardboard piece painted to look like the dark circular opening of a tomb

Costumes: Costumes for everyone are optional. If used, consider simple pieces such as sashes and shoulder pieces.
      A white robe for the angel

(Children take their places on the platform. Keep enough space in front for the "donkey ride.")

CHILD 1: Hosanna! Hosanna! The people all cried
      As Jesus took a donkey ride.

(A JESUS *character rides another child for a short distance while the rest of the children wave palm branches and shout "Hosanna!" Then, group sings "Hosanna.")*

CHILD 2 *(dressed as an angel):*
      "He is alive," an angel said,
      "Jesus lives, He is not dead."

(The child in angel white stands beside a dark "tomb" opening painted on a large piece of cardboard that can simply be brought onstage and held in place by an adult helper. One or two young children appear to be peeking in when the angel says her lines. After the lines, group sings "Clap Your Hands.")

ALL: Jesus loves me, this I know,
      Easter morning shows me so.

(All sing "Jesus Loves the Little Ones," then leave the platform.)

The Praise Parade
A presentation for Palm Sunday
by Nancy Gordon, Dennis and Nan Allen
adapted by Debbie Goodwin

Theme: Palm Sunday
Scripture: Matthew 21:1-2, 6-9
Uses: Palm Sunday
Music: "Easter Praise Parade" and "Here Comes the King"
Cast: NARRATOR: An adult
A large group of children
CHEERLEADER 1 and 2
Props: Bible
Parade streamers, banners, etc.
Signs that read "Good News," "He Is Alive," "Jesus," etc.
Pom-poms for cheerleaders
Cymbals, drums, and other rhythm or percussion instruments, optional

(NARRATOR *enters.*)

NARRATOR *(reading from the Bible):* "As they approached Jerusalem and came to Bethphage on the Mount of Olives, Jesus sent two disciples, saying to them, 'Go to the village ahead of you, and at once you will find a donkey tied there, with her colt by her. Untie them and bring them to me. . . .' The disciples went and did as Jesus had instructed them. They brought the donkey and the colt, placed their cloaks on them, and Jesus sat on them. A very large crowd . . . cut branches from the trees and spread them on the road. The crowds that went ahead of him and those that followed shouted. 'Hosanna, to the Son of David!' 'Blessed is he who comes in the name of the Lord!' 'Hosanna in the highest!'"

(Closes the Bible and speaks directly to the audience)
Now, that was a parade, for sure. Today, we see few palm branches at parades. And certainly no one lays down his Gap jeans jacket for anybody to walk on. Instead, you see streamers and banners, bands and other noisemakers. If we had a parade for Jesus today, it might look something like this . . .

(Children are ready on cue to make their entrance from the back of the auditorium. As soon as the music to "Easter Praise Parade" begins, the children enter singing and carrying flags, signs, streamers, and banners. They congregate on the platform, marching in time while finishing the music.)

ALL *(singing):*
Now it's time for a celebration
It's the Easter Praise Parade.
Celebrate His resurrection.
It's an Easter Praise Parade.
Jesus is alive, and we're here to sing His praise.
Come and join the celebration.
It's an Easter Praise Parade!

Shout for joy, you children, for the stone is rolled away.
Shout for joy, for Jesus Christ is risen from the grave.

(Repeat "Now it's time for a celebration . . .")

Shout for joy, you children, tell everyone you see.
Shout for joy that Jesus Christ has won the victory.
Triumphantly He rode into the city,
And then He suffered at the hands of men.
He hung upon a cross at the hill of Calvary,
And then from death He came to life again.

(Repeat "Now it's time for a celebration . . .")

CHEERLEADER 1 *(coming to the front of the group to lead the cheer):* Ready? OK!

ALL *(with great enthusiasm and rehearsed cheerleading motions):*
Rah . . . rah . . . cheer . . . cheer . . .
Jesus Christ is coming near.
Rah . . . rah . . . hoo-ray
Jesus Christ is on His way.

CHEERLEADER 1 *(solo):* J . . . E . . . S-U-S

CHEERLEADER 2 *(echoing):* J . . . E . . . S-U-S

ALL: J . . . E . . . S-U-S. Jesus!

CHEERLEADER 1: Jesus!

CHEERLEADER 2: Jesus!

ALL: Jesus! *(All jump up and down and continue cheering by saying, "Yeah! All right! Jesus!" etc.)*

(Prepare to sing "Here Comes the King.")

Holy Week Live
An interactive story using rhythmic repetition
by Dave Tippett

Theme: Easter

Uses: Any Easter emphasis or other occasion for retelling the last week of Jesus' life on earth

Music: "Jesus Is Alive and Doin' Well," "He's Alive"

Cast: NARRATOR: an adult with good rhythm and concentration
　　　　PRAISERS: at least 2 from the palm branch procession
　　　　A BLIND ONE: who now sees
　　　　A HEALED ONE: from broken limbs
　　　　MERCHANT: who sells sacrificial lambs
　　　　LAMB: who "baas" for attention
　　　　WIDOW: with her last coins
　　　　DISCIPLES 1 and 2: arguing about who's best
　　　　DISCIPLES 3 and 4: discussing stinky feet
　　　　PETER: when he denied Jesus
　　　　JESUS: twice appears
　　　　THE CROSS: pantomimed
　　　　MARY: announcing the Resurrection
　　　　TRUMPETER: also announcing the Resurrection

Special Note:
This is a storytelling technique using rhythm and action. Each character has a line and action to deliver within two rounds of a three-beat count. The audience sustains the rhythm

with a continuous stomp-stomp-clap. The actions are simple so that they can be repeated in a fairly mechanical way in time with a beat. A few lines require two actors. (See MERCHANT and LAMB.) The following chart demonstrates how to coordinate the actors' lines and audience's rhythm. Boldfaced words receive the accent.

	Stomp	Stomp	**Clap**	Stomp	Stomp	**Clap**
PRAISERS	Praise	Him!	**Praise Him!**	We	gonna	**praise Him!**
BLIND	Now	I	**see!**	Now	I	see!
HEALED	New	**arm!**	*(beat)*	*(beat)*	New	leg!
MERCHANT	Ching	Ching		Ching	Ching	
LAMB			**Baaa**			**Baaa**
WIDOW	Last	**coin**	*(beat)*	*(beat)*	for	You!
DISCIPLES 1 & 2	I'm	the	**best!**	You're	the	rest!
DISCIPLE 3	My	feet	*(beat)*	*(beat)*	don't	**stink!**
DISCIPLE 4	Your	feet	*(beat)*	*(beat)*	do	**stink!**
PETER	Don't	know	**Him!**	Don't	know	Him!
MARY	He	lives!		He	lives!	
TRUMPETER			**Ta-ta-da!**			**Ta-ta-da!**
JESUS	Spread	the	**news!**	Spread	the	news!

(NARRATOR *enters to stand center stage, and all participants, except* JESUS *and the* CROSS, *enter to stand in a line at the back of the platform. As needed, they will move closer to the front to perform their rhythmic action.*)

NARRATOR: This is a special telling of the story of Jesus and what He did during His last week with us before He went to heaven. To tell the story, I'm going to need some help from the audience. During our story, you must do this (*demonstrates stomping foot twice and clapping once to produce a stomp-stomp-clap cadence*). OK, now you try. (*Audience tries while* NARRATOR *teases the audience about their rhythm until everyone is keeping the correct cadence.*) Now, it's very important that you keep doing this all the way through the story. My helpers (*points to the line of children*) will do the rest. Everybody ready? Let's begin. (*Starts the audience with their stomp-stomp-clap cadence.*)

NARRATOR: As Jesus entered Jerusalem, many, many people came to see him and worship him.

(PRAISERS *step forward to deliver their line and action.*)

PRAISERS: Praise Him! Praise Him! We gonna praise Him! (*One child waves the other child's arm like a palm branch.* NARRATOR *pauses for a few repetitions, making sure the children and audience have set a good rhythmic pattern.*)

NARRATOR: As Jesus traveled through the city those first few days, He healed many people. He made blind men and women see! He helped people who had other physical problems too.

(The Blind *and* Healed *characters step forward to say their lines simultaneously.)*

Blind: Now I see! Now I see! *(Hides eyes on "Now I" and throws open hands on "see," keeping the same rhythm as the audience)*

Healed: New arm—new leg. *(Holds healed arm out on "New arm" and points to healed leg on "New leg")*

Narrator: When Jesus began to teach and preach, the religious leaders watched Him with anger because Jesus made them look bad. Every time they tried to challenge Jesus, He would win the argument, and they had to go away. Early in the week, at the Temple, many merchants gathered to sell lambs to worshipers for their sacrifices. The merchants made extra money by overcharging the people.

*(*Merchant *and* Lamb *step forward to deliver their line and action.)*

Merchant: Ching, ching *(With one hand extended, pantomimes letting two coins drop)*

Lamb *(on all fours until after the* Merchant*'s ching-ching when he gets up on "hind feet" and says . . .):* Baaa!

Narrator: When Jesus saw what was going on in His Father's house, He was very upset. He could not allow these people to use His Father's house as a place of business. He went in and knocked over the merchants' tables and drove out their lambs. Jesus knew that the leaders were out to make trouble for Him . . . but He also knew His Father, God, had a plan for Him. *(Pause briefly)* Back in the Temple that day, Jesus saw a widow give the last of her money to God. Jesus said that she had given much more than anyone else because she gave all she had with a good attitude, an attitude that put God first.

*(*Widow *steps forward to share her line and action.)*

Widow: Last coin—for you. *(*Widow *says "Last coin" while reaching into an imaginary purse and says "for You" while holding coin to the sky. Repeat in time with audience's cadence.)*

Narrator: Later in the week, Jesus' friends prepared for a *big* supper on Thursday night. As they gathered, these friends started arguing about who was most important.

*(*Disciples 1 *and* 2 *step forward to share their line and action.)*

Disciples 1 and 2 *(together):* I'm the best—you're the rest. *(Each points to self on "I'm the best" and the other person on "you're the rest.")*

Narrator: Jesus told them that the most humble are the *best* in God's eyes. Then, He demonstrated what that meant by washing the disciples' feet. He wanted to show them how to be servants to each other.

*(*Disciples 3 *and* 4 *step forward to say their lines simultaneously.)*

Disciple 3 *(sitting in a chair or on a stool):* My feet—don't stink. *(Holds out foot while saying "My feet," and shakes head on "don't stink")*

Disciple 4: Your feet—do stink. *(Standing beside* Disciple 3, *points to* Disciple 3*'s foot with extended thumb on "His feet" and holds nose with other hand on "do stink")*

Narrator: Jesus told them to remember Him as they shared bread and wine. That's when Judas left to betray Jesus. After Jesus prayed to His Father about what was going to happen, He was arrested and sent to jail. Peter, one of Jesus' friends, was waiting around a big campfire outside the jail. Someone asked him if he knew Jesus. Peter denied knowing Him because he was afraid of being arrested too.

*(*Peter *steps forward to join rhythmic line.)*

PETER: Don't know—Him. *(Shakes head on "Don't know" and turns his head to point to an imaginary Jesus on "Him.")*

NARRATOR: Wow! *(Referring to the still chanting kids)* A lot happened that week! But . . . the most important part of the story still has to be told, so everyone, FREEZE. (NARRATOR *addresses this first to the actors and then motions to the audience to stop also.)*

NARRATOR *(after a short pause to let the silence settle):* On the Friday of the last week of Jesus' life on earth, the religious leaders wanted to make sure that Jesus would never bother them again. They got the Romans to agree to have Jesus put to death.

(JESUS *comes to center stage and stands with arms to his side, letting his head hang down. The* CROSS *comes to center stage to stand behind* JESUS *with arms down but head up.)*

NARRATOR: Jesus was nailed to a cross. (CROSS *holds arms out straight while* JESUS *remains in same pose with arms and head down.)*

NARRATOR: There, God provided forgiveness for every bad attitude and action committed against God. On the Cross, Jesus took the punishment for all our sin, because He loved us enough to make a way for us to get back to God. When Jesus was about to die, He said, "Father, take Me in Your arms!" And God did.

(JESUS *slowly raises his head to look up and makes a slow exit. The* CROSS *remains with arms outstretched for a count to 3, then exits too.)*

NARRATOR: Jesus' body was put into a tomb, and His friends were very sad. Many looked back on the week before and remembered Him and everything that happened. On the third day, several of Jesus' friends came to the tomb to find Him gone! He had risen from the dead! (NARRATOR *motions the audience to resume their stomp-stomp-clap cadence.)*

(MARY *and* TRUMPETER *step forward to deliver their parts.)*

MARY: He lives! *(Begins with head down, and raises head to say "He lives!")*

TRUMPETER *(holds imaginary horn down on* MARY's *"He lives," then raises it to make the trumpet call):* Ta-ta-da!

NARRATOR: After that . . . *(motions to all rhythmic participants to resume their lines and actions)* Jesus appeared to many people before He went to heaven. He left a very important message to all His followers:

JESUS *(reenters to stand at center stage):* Spread the news. *(With one hand, palm up at waist level, the other hand, also palm up, makes a large sweeping gesture.)*

(NARRATOR *begins moving from group to group. After commenting on the action, motions action to stop. Participants freeze midline or midaction.)*

NARRATOR: Today, we looked back on Holy Week and saw how people reacted to Jesus. Isn't it interesting that people react to Jesus the same way today? *(Goes to* PRAISERS) Today, some continue to praise Him for the moment.

(NARRATOR *motions the* PRAISERS *to freeze and goes to* BLIND *and* HEALED.)*

NARRATOR: Some continue to receive a special healing touch from Jesus.

(NARRATOR *motions* BLIND *and* HEALED *to stop and goes to* MERCHANT *and* LAMB.)*

NARRATOR: Some still do things in His name just to make money.

(Stops MERCHANT *and* LAMB, *then goes to* WIDOW)

NARRATOR: Many people who believe in Jesus are good examples.

(Stops WIDOW *and goes to* DISCIPLES 1-4)

NARRATOR: Of course, some hear His lessons but still don't understand.

(Stops DISCIPLES *and goes to* PETER)

NARRATOR: Many continue to deny their relationship with Him.

(Stops PETER *and goes to* MARY *and* TRUMPETER)

NARRATOR: Many continue to marvel at Jesus and His victory . . . .

(Stops MARY *and* TRUMPETER *and goes to* JESUS)

NARRATOR: Listen to His commandments.

(This time NARRATOR *does not stop* JESUS.)

(All actors exit in haphazard order, leaving JESUS *saying "Spread the news!"* NARRATOR *stops the audience cadence to say last line.)*

NARRATOR: I wonder where YOU fit in? *(Exits leaving* JESUS *alone onstage. He repeats his line about 3 times then freezes for a count of 5 and exits.)*

(Transition to "Jesus Is Alive and Doin' Well": Rather than have JESUS *exit, allow him to freeze in place for a brief time, and then have the children who will sing take their places quickly to begin this upbeat song.*

(For a more meditative ending, use "He's Alive" as a round. Divide the choir into three groups. Have participants from the first group gather and sing. The second group gathers while the first group sings. The third group gathers while the second and first group sing. End with everyone raising an excited shout: He's alive!)

Helpful Hints

▸ Make sure the children can sustain the appropriate rhythm before adding narration.

▸ To increase participation, give lines and actions to different groups of children. Arrange them in an interesting way on the stage, making use of raised stage areas (risers, stairs, etc.) if possible.

▸ Encourage each new group to deliver their lines loud enough to be heard *over* the rest. Practice appropriate volume levels so that the audience can understand all narration.

▸ Play a game of freeze to help participants find good freeze positions. Ask everyone to say his or her lines and complete his or her action while standing in a circle. Director stands in the center. At different times, the Director shouts "freeze." Talk about what makes a good freeze picture.

▸ With a few adaptations, use this as a storytelling technique for children's church. Ask for volunteers to deliver the rhythmic lines and action. Ask the rest to provide the stomp-stomp-clap cadence. Preselect the participants for Jesus and the Cross. Divide the group into sections. Rehearse the rhythmic lines and then tell the story.

Mother's Day

Sharing Love

A simple four-line piece for young children

by Iris Gray Dowling

Theme: Mothers, Mother's Day
Uses: To honor mothers
Music: "A Happy Home"
Cast: For young children participants divided into two groups

(All enter and stand as two groups.)

GROUP 1: To all the mothers gathered here,
Listen to what we say:

GROUP 2: We want to share our love with you,
  No one cares your way.

ALL: We love you! *(All throw a kiss.)*
  Have a Happy Mother's Day!

(All exit.)

What Mother Means to Me
A short piece for various ages
by Iris Gray Dowling

Theme: Mothers, Mother's Day
Uses: To honor mothers
Music: "A Happy Home"
Cast: May use all ages or one age-group. Suitable for young children and early elementary.
  3 solo speaking parts

(Children enter and take their places at the front of the platform. Solo speakers stand within easy access to a microphone.)

ALL: On this day we'd like to say
  What Mother means to me—

CHILD 1: A heart of love.

(All draw hearts in the air using two fingers, drawing the symmetrical sides.)

CHILD 2: A happy kiss.

(All put palm to lips and throw imaginary kisses.)

CHILD 3: A great big hug.

(All hug themselves with both arms.)

ALL: All these and more are what I see.
  Thank you, Mother.
  Have a happy day.

A Great Big Thank You!
An acted-out rhyme for late elementary girls
by Rena Myers

Theme: Mothers, Mother's Day
Use: A mother-daughter occasion or other occasion to honor mothers
Music: "Just Say It"
Cast: Late elementary grade girls divided into 4 groups
Props: Cheerleading pom-poms
  Large calendar
  An extra large banner prepared on a roll of shelf paper or art paper that reads: HAPPY MOTHER'S DAY!

(Help each group to identify a freeze pose that relates to their lines. Participants walk onstage and take their freeze poses. Each group breaks the pose to say lines, then returns to the freeze until they break the freeze for the last lines at the end.)

GROUP 1 *(expressing worry and biting nails):*
    You calm our fears,

GROUP 2 *(holding pom-poms as if in the middle of a cheer):*
    You lead our cheers,

GROUP 3 *(holding a large calendar and looking at it, pointing to different days):*
    You mold our plans,

GROUP 4 *(holding hands by couples as if for encouragement):*
    You hold our hands.

GROUPS 1 and 3 *(break freeze):* You're always there.

GROUPS 2 and 4 *(break freeze):* You always care.

ALL: That's why we say . . .

(One girl takes the beginning of the rolled banner and walks to the other side of the group, unrolling the message so that all can read it while the group says it.)

ALL: HAPPY MOTHER'S DAY!

(Bow and exit)

(Transition to "Just Say It": Stop the dialogue after GROUPS *2 and 4 say "You always care," and lead into the song "Just Say It." Look for some creative motions to help deliver the message of the song.)*

Doing Our Part
A fun tribute with creative props for late elementary participants
by Margaret Primrose

Theme: Mothers, Mother's Day
Uses: To honor mothers at a service or other celebration
Music: "Just Say It"
Cast: 9 speakers
        As many other late elementary boys and girls as desired
Props: A few dishes that stack easily
        Dirty socks
        A pillow
        A bucket of blocks
        Child's toy
        Dog dish or package of dog food
        Broom
        Schoolbooks

(Participants enter and stand with their backs to audience. Participants turn to face audience and say their line in keeping with the rhythm of the piece. After the unison line, each returns to a freeze pose, this time facing the audience until the end.)

SPEAKER 1 *(with a stack of dishes):* Dirty dishes . . .

SPEAKER 2 *(holding dirty socks):* Dirty socks . . .

SPEAKER 3 *(fluffing a pillow):* Unmade beds . . .

SPEAKER 4 *(holding a bucket of blocks):* And scattered blocks;

SPEAKERS 1, 2, 3, 4: Moms don't like them. What can we say?

SPEAKER 5 *(holding a child's toy):* Being a mother is not all play.

SPEAKERS 5, 6 *(speaking to each other as if trying to solve a problem):* How can we help to even the score?

SPEAKER 7 *(holding a dog dish or dog food):* Feed the dog . . .

SPEAKER 8 *(sweeping with a broom):* And sweep the floor;

SPEAKER 9 *(holding a stack of schoolbooks):* Do our homework with a smile.

ALL *(all break freeze to say in unison):* And tell Mom "Thank you" once in a while.

My Mother Is
A rhymed piece with costumes chosen by the children
by Martha Bolton

Theme: Mothers, Mother's Day

Uses: Any occasion to honor mothers

Music: "Just Say It"

Cast: For 10 late elementary speakers

For boys and girls of various ages. If chosen for an all-women event, use all girls.

Costumes: Each participant dresses for the role of the part to be played. Let the children be creative and suggest their own costumes.

Props: A stack of books

Car keys and city map

Cleaning paraphernalia such as pail and mop and feather duster

Stop sign and police whistle

Piece of clothing with needle and long thread for sewing

Bible

Garden tools

First-aid kit

Mixing bowl and spoon

Clown nose made from a small red soft foam ball

(Participants enter and stand in a tight horizontal line at the front of the platform. Use two standing microphones, if possible. Odd numbers use microphone 1 and even numbers use microphone 2. Always keep two people at the microphones to make for a smooth presentation.)

SPEAKER 1 *(balancing a large stack of books):*

My mother is a teacher,
No summer off has she!
She is my live-in tutor
And does it all for free!

SPEAKER 2 *(holding keys and city map):*

My mother is a chauffeur.
She takes me wherever I go,
Even when she'd rather be
Asleep in bed, I know!

SPEAKER 3 *(carrying ironing and cleaning paraphernalia):*

My mommy does the ironing,
The washing, and the floors!
The cleaning and the dishes
Are more of her FUN chores!

SPEAKER 4 *(carrying a stop sign and whistle):*
My mommy's a cop—
When I fight, she says—STOP! *(Holds out stop sign)*

SPEAKER 5 *(using large hand motions to sew a button on a blouse):*
My mother is a seamstress,
    Sewing buttons and bows.
And she doesn't even get the thanks
    For everything she sews!

SPEAKER 6 *(holding a Bible):*
My mother is a preacher,
    But Pastor _____ she's not! *(Fill in pastor's name)*
He only gets ONE HOUR to preach;
    All day and night she's got!

SPEAKER 7 *(carrying gardening tools):*
My mommy is a gardener,
    Although her thumb is brown. *(Holds up a brown thumb or dead plant)*
She's got the most ambition
    Of anyone in town!

SPEAKER 8 *(holding a first-aid kit):*
My mommy is a nurse.
She fixes all my little hurts! *(Shows a large Band-Aid on her elbow)*

SPEAKER 9 *(pretending to stir something in a mixing bowl with a wooden spoon):*
My mommy's a cook
    And a baker and chef.
I always clean the plate—
(in a loud whisper) It's just that the
    Vegetables are always left!

SPEAKER 10 *(holds the clown nose behind back):*
My mom is a . . . *(puts clown nose on)*
    clown.
She makes me laugh when I am
    down!

ALL: HAPPY MOTHER'S DAY, MOM!

(Transition to "Just Say It": Stop the dialogue after SPEAKER 10, *and have the combined children's choir sing "Just Say It." After the song, everyone shouts "Happy Mother's Day, Mom!")*

More Mother's Day Ideas

▸ Have children prepare thank-you notes to give to mothers at the end of their presentation.
▸ Have children present a flower to each mother.
▸ Ask a photographer to be available to take pictures of moms with their children.

Promotion Day

Moving On
A graded Promotion Day program
by Debbie Salter Goodwin

New beginnings need celebrations. It is true even if the new beginning means moving to a new grade or class. The following is a fun way to recognize a year of growth and development as well as commit to another year of even more. Find your own ways to personalize and adapt to your specific context.

Seat children in groups with their teachers. Identify a LEADER who will introduce each children's group and narrate transitions. Study each presentation for necessary props and speaking parts. Decide whether you will recognize children individually or by groups. If you present certificates, consider presenting them privately in classrooms.

Growing

A promotion presentation for young children
by Debbie Salter Goodwin

Theme: Promotion, growth
Use: Promotion Day or end of the year or celebration for children
Music: "I'm Special"
Cast: The teacher(s) and children from this age-group
Props: None are necessary. However, to add interest, the kindergartners can hold rulers, yardsticks, and tape measures and act out measuring each other.

ALL: We have been growing this year.
See, we are this tall. *(Participants either place hands on top of heads to accentuate height or use measuring tools to measure each other.)*

TEACHER: Not all the growth is measured in inches. The best growth comes in verses:

(ALL *repeat one or two memory verses.*)

ALL: We have been growing this year
Even when we aren't growing here *(put hands on top of heads as if to measure)*, we want it to show here. *(All point to their hearts.)*

LEADER: This _____ class certainly has been growing with _____ *(insert name of teacher)* as their teacher. We have _____ *(insert number)* class members who will be promoted to _____. They are _____, _____, and _____ *(give names)*.

(The young children leave, and the next class takes their place on the stage.)

Primary[1] Spellers

An early elementary promotion presentation
by Debbie Salter Goodwin

Theme: Promotion, growth
Uses: Promotion
Music: "Teach Me, Lord"
Cast: 13 children, 7 who say a line and hold a letter. The other 6 hold a prop or demonstrate an activity
Props: 7 signs with large colorful letters spelling **P-R-I-M-A-R-Y**
        Picture of Jesus
        Bible
        Craft project
        Bible verse memory poster

---

1. You may substitute the appropriate name or grade and make your own acrostic with the letters, with or without rhyme.

(Primaries walk to assigned places on the stage. Seven children on the front row hold letter signs turned so that the audience can't read them.)

LEADER *(as primaries get into place):* Primary stands for first, fundamental, basic, and certainly that describes our primary class taught by _____ *(insert teacher's name).*
Here are the first and second graders to share some things from their year.

CHILD 1 *(holds up "P"):*
P is for pictures of Jesus, you see.

CHILD 2 *(holds up a picture of Jesus)*

CHILD 3 *(holds up "R"):*
R is for reading what He did for me.

CHILD 4 *(holds up a Bible as if reading it)*

CHILD 5 *(holds up "I"):*
I is for interesting things we can make.

CHILD 6 *(holds up a craft project from the year)*

CHILD 7 *(holds up "M"):*
M is for meeting new friends by handshake.

CHILD 8 and 9 *(shake hands)*

CHILD 10 *(holds up "A"):*
A is for answering questions for review. *(Several children raise their hands as if waiting to be called upon.)*

CHILD 11 *(holds "R"):*
R is for remembering Bible verses by cue.

CHILD 12 *(holds up Bible verse memory poster from the year)*

CHILD 13 *(holds up "Y"):*
Y is for yes; our answer for sure,
If you want us to take you
On a primary class tour.

(All shake their heads yes with enthusiasm.)

LEADER: We are proud of our primaries, and especially proud of the second graders who will be promoted. *(Either recognize them individually by name or ask the group to step forward.)* Thank you, primaries. We look forward to another good year.

(Primaries leave the stage, and the next group walks to the stage.)

Body Language

A promotion presentation for the middle elementary grades
by Debbie Salter Goodwin

Theme: Promotion, growth
Uses: Promotion, Sunday School emphasis
Music: "We Are God's Children"
Cast: All 3rd and 4th grade
Production Notes: Middlers[2] who create the letters of their name with their bodies. As much as possible, use everyone to help form the body letters. Here's how:

---

2. Substitute with the name of any class and invent your own way of forming the letters.

M: Two face each other and make the dip of the M by dropping their arms and touching hands.

I: Child stands straight and tall.

D: Child stands straight, arms down. Another makes the round of D by arching body outward, touching partner's head with hands and placing feet as close to partner's feet as possible. Another two children repeat this letter.

L: Child stands straight, arms down. Another sits against the legs of partner, feet extended.

E: Child stands, sideways to audience with one arm extended straight. Partner sits, back against partner's legs, one arm extended at head level, feet extended.

R: Child stands sideways to audience with one leg extended in a step. Partner stands behind, making a circle with arms.

A CHEERLEADER to lead the cheer

Props: None unless you want to give the Cheerleader some pom-poms.

LEADER: Middlers are our energetic third and fourth graders. They are taught by _____ (*insert teacher's name*). To prove they are the most energetic of our children's department, they have a cheer for us:

CHEERLEADER: Give me an M! (*Two children step out to form M.*)

ALL: M!

CHEERLEADER: Give me an I! (*One person steps out to form I.*)

ALL: I!

CHEERLEADER: Give me a D! (*Two children step out to form D.*)

ALL: D!

CHEERLEADER: Give me another D! (*Two more children step out to form a D.*)

ALL: D!

CHEERLEADER: Give me an L! (*Two children step out to form L.*)

ALL: L!

CHEERLEADER: Give me an E! (*Two children step out to form E.*)

ALL: E!

CHEERLEADER: Give me an R! (*Two children step out to form R.*)

ALL: R!

CHEERLEADER: What do you have?

ALL: Energetic . . .

CHEERLEADER: What do you have?

ALL: Enthusiastic . . .

CHEERLEADER: What do you have?

ALL: Exciting . . .

CHEERLEADER: What do you have?

ALL: Middlers!

CHEERLEADER: Who are they?

ALL: Middlers!

CHEERLEADER: Tell me again!

ALL: Middlers!

(All letter-makers break letter poses and jump up and down with enthusiastic celebration!)

LEADER: All that energy and enthusiasm has been focused in good ways this year. We are happy that *(give names)* are being promoted to the preteen class. Let's congratulate this special achievement!

(Middlers leave the stage, and the next group takes its place on the stage.)

Good Cooking
A late elementary promotion presentation
by Debbie Salter Goodwin

Theme: Promotion, growth
Uses: Promotion or Sunday School emphasis
Music: "Saints Society"
Cast: All preteens[3] with 6 who have a speaking line
Props: Alarm clock
  Several strips of paper
  Game boards and spinners
  Sign: 9:30-10:30
  Various kitchen tools: bowls, wooden spoons, measuring cups, etc.
Costumes: Participants wear aprons, chef hats, and carry appropriate cooking tools.

LEADER: Here come the fifth and sixth graders. They are a mix of very interesting young people who know how to cook up something special every week. They are coming to share their recipe with you.

(Enter dressed in aprons and chef hats and carrying appropriate cooking tools.)

CHILD 1: Take one fun-loving and caring teacher named *(insert name of teacher)*.

(Two children pull teacher to a place in the center of the group.)

CHILD 2 *(holding an alarm clock or timer)*: Add an hour of looking at how Jesus wants us to live. *(Sets alarm or timer for an hour.)*

CHILD 3: Sprinkle generously with questions that our teacher didn't prepare answers for.

(Several children take strips of paper and throw them around.)

CHILD 4: Mix in plenty of time for fun and games.

(A few children hold up game boards and spinners from past class activities.)

CHILD 5 *(holds a sign 9:30-10:30)*: Bake from 9:30 to 10:30 every Sunday morning.

CHILD 6: Then, you'll have a class every fifth and sixth grader will want to be a part of!

Performance Idea

Instead of using music after each group's presentation, consider having the children sing either "We Are God's Children" or "We Are the Children."

---

3. Or substitute another division, grade, or class. Make other substitutions to fit your specific situation.

(When the last CHILD *finishes the line, all take a crazy pose until those to be promoted are introduced.)*

LEADER: We are very proud of our fifth and sixth graders. We are especially proud of the sixth graders who are ready to be promoted into the Youth Department. I would like *(insert appropriate name of youth worker)* to come forward and officially welcome these new students into the youth program.

Father's Day

Just Bragging About My Dad

A piece with easy props that help seven speakers praise fathers
by Margaret Primrose

Theme: Fathers, Father's Day
Uses: Father's Day or other father-son occasion
Music: "Lead the Way"
Cast: 7 solo late elementary speakers
Props: A toy or other item, rigged so that a piece comes off to appear broken
> A wrench
> Sports page
> Maps, charts, and/or graphs
> Bible
> A tie

Costumes: CHILD 2 wears overalls.
> CHILD 4 wears sports T-shirt and cap

CHILD 1 *(holding the toy or other item before it "breaks")*: My dad can fix just anything.

(Looks at the object as a piece comes off and falls to the floor) Well, almost!

CHILD 2 *(in overalls with grease on face and wrench in hand)*: He works on cars . . .

CHILD 3 *(struggling to open a jar)*: . . . and opens jars.

CHILD 4 *(wearing sports T-shirt and cap, holding sports page)*: My daddy knows all kind of facts, Like baseball scores.

CHILD 5 *(said with confidence unrolling a map or graph)*: He studies maps and charts and graphs . . . and albacores?

(Scratches his head and looks at the others who raise their hands in an I-don't-know gesture)

CHILD 6 *(holding Bible)*:
My daddy goes to Sunday School
Every week.

CHILD 7: He says it's more important
Than physique. *(Shows muscles)*

CHILD 8: I'm growing up to be like him
When I'm a man.

Quick Tip Be sensitive to children whose dads aren't present or those who do not have Christian role models from their fathers. Find a way to remind everyone that while dads are important, it's even more important for all of us to grow up like our Heavenly Father.

Instead of ending with "Lead the Way," use this transition to "We Are the Children."

SPEAKER: While we celebrate the men we call fathers, we also think about another Father on this day, our Heavenly Father. We are His children too!

(Attempting to tie a tie but can't)
> I guess I have a ways to go . . .
> But that's my plan.

F Is for Father

An acrostic for Father's Day
by Wanda E. Brunstetter

Theme: Fathers, Father's Day
Uses: Father's Day or any father-son occasion
Music: "Lead the Way, Dad"
Cast: For early and/or late elementary
> 6 letter holders who speak a line
> 6 sign holders
> As many others as desired

Props: 6 large cutout, colorful letters
> 6 poster signs with the words: Fearless, Awesome, Truthful, Helpful, Energetic, Remark-
> able
> Make sure that props are large enough for people to see from the back.

(Children with letters stand in front with letters hidden. The rest, including sign holders, group themselves behind the letter holders).

CHILD 1 *(holding the F):*
> F is for **fearless**—that's my dad.

CHILD 2 *(holding the A):*
> A is for **awesome**—the best father anybody had.

CHILD 3 *(holding the T):*
> T is for **truthful**—I know I can count on him.

CHILD 4 *(holding the H):*
> H is for **helpful**—he taught me to swim.

CHILD 5 *(holding the E):*
> E is for **energetic**—to keep up with me.

CHILD 6 *(holding the R):*
> R is for **remarkable**—and no one will disagree.

ALL: If we put the letters together,
> Then we have to also add
> **FATHER** is a . . .

(Designated children hold up the appropriate sign as the group shouts the word. Place these in random order throughout the group to give a popcorn effect as they appear.)

ALL: Fearless
> Awesome
> Truthful
> Helpful
> Energetic
> Remarkable man we call Dad.

Short Subjects
Quick two-line openers for a Father's Day feature
by Martha Bolton

Theme: Fathers, Father's Day
Uses: Father's Day or other father-son occasion
Music: "Lead the Way"
Cast: 2 early or late elementary boys
  Teen
  Dad with a strong back
Props: Car keys
  A fishing pole and other fishing accessories
  A small minnow-looking fish
Costumes: Boy 2 wears oversized men's clothing and shoes
  Boy 3 wears fishing clothes

(Participants enter to deliver lines and then exit.)

1: The Ride

Boy 1 *(enters riding his father's back):* When you're small, you borrow Dad's back and go for a ride!

Teen *(enters holding car keys):* When you're a teen, you borrow his car and do the same!

2: The Shoes

Boy 2 *(enters dressed in Dad's clothes and shoes that are too big for him):* I just have one thing to say, Dad. I could never fill your shoes!

3: The Fishy Story

Boy 3 *(enters in fishing clothes with "minnow" hidden):* Dad, remember when you went fishing and snagged the BIG one, but you said you had to let it go or it would sink the boat? Well, I want you to know we found it. *(Holds up a minnow)*

More Ideas to Celebrate Parents

▸ Use children to greet mothers and fathers on Sunday morning by having them place a happy face sticker on each parent.

▸ Collect baby photos of the mothers/fathers in your church, and put them on the church bulletin board. Have church members guess who they are. Provide a voting ballot with the names of their children. Award the winner with the most correct answers a special photo album for their children's pictures.

▸ Have the several children dress up in their parent's uniform or work clothes. Work with them to finish this sentence: I am the son/daughter of a _____ and that means _____ for me.

Fourth of July ✺

God's Declaration of Our Dependence
Quotes from historical figures emphasize the Bible's importance
by Daisy Jenney Clay

Theme: The Bible and its place in American history

Scripture: 2 Timothy 3:16-17

Uses: Any patriotic celebration, Christian school program

Music: "Teach Me, Lord"

Cast: 13 late elementary children who will memorize or read an explanation or famous quotation from a famous person

Props: Bible

> Best-seller list or poster of the top 10 best-sellers
>
> 13 scrolls

Costumes: While none are necessary, they will add interest. Look up pictures of these famous people in an encyclopedia, and explore some easy ways to represent the historical characters through costumes.

(Children enter and take places across the platform. Consider using two standing microphones and assign each character microphone 1 or 2.)

CHILD 1 *(holding a Bible):* My dad told me that the Bible is a best-seller, but that's not why it is the most valuable book in the world.

CHILD 2 *(showing a best-seller list or a poster of the top 10 best-sellers):* Other best-sellers are popular for only a short time, but the Bible has been read and loved for centuries and by people of many countries.

CHILD 3: Most of the great men of our country have valued the Bible. George Washington said, "It is impossible to rightly govern the world without God and the Bible. He is worse than an infidel who does not read his Bible."

CHILD 4: Our second president, John Adams, wrote, "The Bible is the best Book in the world." He read a chapter from the Book every day.

CHILD 5: Thomas Jefferson, who wrote our Declaration of Independence, loved his Bible and read it. From him came the words, "I have always said that the study of this sacred volume will make better citizens and better fathers. The Bible makes the best people in the world."

CHILD 6: At one time, Lincoln said, "I am profitably engaged in reading the Bible. It is God's best gift to man."

CHILD 7: Our more recent presidents were of the same opinion. In New England, you may be shown a spot in the woods where Theodore Roosevelt often used to go to quietly read the Bible. His sister, in writing about him, tells us that he knew a great deal of Scripture by memory.

CHILD 8: The later President Franklin Delano Roosevelt declared, "If men and nations would return to the teachings of the Sermon on the Mount, there would not be all these troubled times in the world today."

CHILD 9: Woodrow Wilson, who was president of a university before he was president of our country, said, "No one is really educated who is not familiar with the Bible."

CHILD 10: President Herbert Hoover wrote, "Reading the Bible is a necessity of American life."

CHILD 11: We have all heard about Douglas MacArthur who helped win the war with Japan and later was head of the army group that went into Japan to aid them in recovering from the effects of the war. With all these great responsibilities, he told us, "Believe me, never a night goes by, be I ever so tired, but I read the Word of God before I go to bed."

CHILD 12: Most of us know about Captain Eddie Rickenbacker and how he was afloat in a small life raft for many days upon the empty vastness of the Pacific Ocean. Afterward he said, "Probably, I would not have survived if it had not been for the strength I received from the Bible."

CHILD 13: "All Scripture is God-breathed and is useful for teaching, rebuking, correcting and training in righteousness, so that the man of God may be thoroughly equipped for every good work" (2 Timothy 3:16-17).

(Transition to "Teach Me, Lord": Ask the following speakers to add these lines at the end to provide the transition to the music.)

CHILD 1: That's why today, we declare our dependence on God.

CHILD 2: We declare our dependence on God's Word

CHILD 13: And our prayer is, teach me, Lord.

(Sing "Teach Me, Lord.")

Thanksgiving

Thank You, God
A simple piece for young children
by Velda Blumhagen

Theme: Thanking God, prayer
Uses: Thanksgiving Day
Music: "God Hears My Prayer"
Cast: 3 or more young children

(Children take their places on the platform.)

ALL *(folding hands):* We'll fold our hands,
    (bowing heads) We'll bow our heads,
    And this is what we pray:
    Thank You, God,
    For love and care
    This glad Thanksgiving Day.

Quick Tip By changing the last line, you can use this piece for more than Thanksgiving. Replace "This glad Thanksgiving Day" with "This happy worship day."

Our Thanks
An acrostic using scripture
by Velda Blumhagen

Theme: Thanking God
Scripture: Genesis 1:31; Psalm 24:1; 91:4; 100:3; 106:1; 144:15; Matthew 5:12; 7:7; 1 John 3:2
Uses: Thanksgiving, call to worship
Music: "Bless the Lord"
Cast: 9 late elementary children who will quote a short scripture verse

Props: Large cutout letters to spell **O-U-R T-H-A-N-K-S**.

(Children take positions in a horizontal line with their backs turned to the audience. When it is a child's turn to speak, he or she turns around to show the letter and share the verse.)

CHILD 1 *(holding the **O**):*
  "O give thanks unto the LORD; for he is good" (Psalm 106:1 [KJV]).

CHILD 2 *(holding the **U**):*
  "Under his wings you will find refuge" (Psalm 91:4).

CHILD 3 *(holding the **R**):*
  "Rejoice and be glad, because great is your reward in heaven" (Matthew 5:12).

CHILD 4 *(holding the **T**):*
  "The earth is the LORD's, and everything in it" (Psalm 24:1).

CHILD 5 *(holding the **H**):*
  "Happy are the people . . . whose God is the LORD" (Psalm 144:15 [NRSV]).

CHILD 6 *(holding the **A**):*
  "And God saw every thing that he had made, and, . . . it was very good" (Genesis 1:31 [KJV]).

CHILD 7 *(holding the **N**):*
  "Now we are children of God, and what we will be has not yet been made known" (1 John 3:2).

CHILD 8 *(holding the **K**):*
  "Know that the LORD is God. It is he who made us" (Psalm 100:3).

CHILD 9 *(holding the **S**):*
  "Seek and you will find; knock and the door will be opened to you" (Matthew 7:7).

ALL: Our thanks to God
  We bring this day.
In love we'll try
  To live His way.

Christmas ❋

A Cradle
A two-line piece for young children
by Mary Ann Green

Theme: Jesus' birth
Uses: To introduce a young children's song
  about the birth of Jesus
Music: "Baby Jesus," "Christ Was Born in
  Bethlehem"
Cast: Any number of young children
Props: Manger with hay
    Baby doll wrapped in cloth.

(Use the whole group to say the two lines. Identify one child to put a Baby Jesus in the manger.)

Quick Tips

▶ **Use one of these short pieces before a suggested song.**

▶ **Use as an Advent presentation on Sunday morning.**

▶ **Use at a Christmas Eve service.**

ALL: In a little manger,
　　Lay a tiny stranger.

We Can
Another two-liner for young children
by Mary Ann Green

Theme: Jesus' birth
Uses: To introduce a song or a short pageant
Music: "O Come, Little Children"
Cast: Any number of young children

(The children enter to recite these two lines before singing a Christmas song.)

ALL: We can tell of Jesus' birth.
　　And how He came to us on earth.

Jesus Joy
A young Mary shares a message of joy
by Robert Colbert

Theme: Jesus' birth
Uses: To introduce a song or short scene
Music: "Baby Jesus"
Cast: Young child to play MARY
Props: A doll wrapped as Baby Jesus
Costume: A robe and headpiece to costume a young MARY

(A young girl enters dressed as Mary, carrying "Baby Jesus.")

MARY: Christ was Mary's baby boy,
　　Born to bring us Jesus joy.

Christmas Questions
A Christmas question and answer between a teacher and young children
by Paul Medford

Theme: Jesus' birth
Uses: A young child's Christmas presentation
Music: "Little Wooly Lamb"
Cast: TEACHER
　　　　Any number of young children
Costumes: Optional: Dress some children as lambs, some as angels, some as shepherds.

(TEACHER may stand or sit in front of children.)

TEACHER: What did the sheep say on the first Christmas?

ALL: Baa, baa, baa.

TEACHER: What did the angel say on the first Christmas?

ALL: Jesus is born.

TEACHER: What did the shepherds say on the first Christmas?

ALL: Let's go to Bethlehem.

TEACHER: What do *we* say this Christmas?

ALL: Love Jesus *(point above)* with all *(with arms out wide)* our hearts *(place hands over hearts).*

A Manger Bed

A short piece for six young children
by Wanda E. Brunstetter

Theme: Jesus' birth

Uses: To introduce a song or present as part of a larger program

Music: "Christ Was Born in Bethlehem"

Cast: 6 solo speakers who are young children or early elementary

Props: Manger
Straw
Crown
Doll wrapped as Baby Jesus

Costume: Optional: biblical costumes

(An empty manger is on the stage. Children take places around the manger.)

CHILD 1 *(standing close to the manger):* Jesus had a manger bed,

CHILD 2: A pillow of straw for His head. *(Places a clump of straw in the manger)*

CHILD 3: He didn't fuss or cry a bit. *(Shakes head)*

CHILD 4: Even though this bed didn't fit. *(Points to the manger)*

CHILD 5: A King who came down to earth. *(Brings a crown from behind his back)*

CHILD 6: Born in a manger—a simple birth. *(Places a wrapped Baby Jesus in the manger)*

Need a Lambskin? Suggest a lamb costume by sewing "wooly" tunics made from fake fur.

Tips for Young Children

▶ Practice with costumes on the stage.
▶ Costume some adults to help young children onstage.
▶ Let the children tell YOU the story before asking them to act it out.
▶ Ask them why they should tell the story again.
▶ Give young children something to do and somewhere to look while onstage.
▶ Don't expect them to stand still.
▶ Keep their segments short.

Happy Birthday

Young children celebrate Jesus' birthday
by Paul M. Miller

Theme: Jesus' birth

Uses: A young child's presentation

Music: "Immanuel, Immanuel"

Cast: Any group of young children

Props: Optional: a real or fake birthday cake with candles

(Children enter to recite or sing the lines while standing around a small table holding a birthday cake.)

ALL: Happy birthday, dear Jesus,
Happy birthday to You.
We love You, dear Jesus,
And You love us too.

A Boy's Gift

A shepherd boy and modern boy share their Christmas gifts

by Timothy Miller

Theme: Christmas

Uses: To introduce a song or present as a part of a longer program

Music: "You Are Lord to Me"

Cast: SHEPHERD BOY

MODERN BOY

Props: A shepherd's staff

A toy lamb

Costume: A shepherd's robe

(Both enter and take their places on opposite sides of the stage.)

SHEPHERD BOY *(carrying the toy lamb):*

If I were a shepherd,
I know what I'd do:
I'd give Jesus my lamb
And be His friend too.

MODERN BOY: Since I'm not a shepherd,
Or a wise man, or king,
I'll give Him myself;
My life I will bring.

(Both boys exit the same way they entered or take their places in a group to sing.)

Christmas Lists

An open-ended conversation about giving

by Paul Miller

Theme: Christmas giving

Uses: An introduction to a song or message about giving

Music: "When He Came," "John 3:16"

Cast: Late elementary

JONI: An expressive girl with a very detailed wish list

TONY: An optimistic boy

Props: 2 long scroll-type Christmas lists that will unroll to the floor when released

A pencil for each actor

(JONI and TONY enter from opposite sides of the stage with long wish lists for Christmas. They speak to themselves and check the items off. They alternate speaking, ignoring the other's presence for a while.)

JONI: Let's see, now, I have my Barbie list, my clothes list . . .

TONY: And I have my Nintendo list, my action figures list, my video list, my . . .

JONI: Now here's my sports equipment list. Let's see, it includes new in-line skates and a blue gymnastics outfit, and . .

TONY: Whew, close call—I almost forgot to add a micro-close-up lens for my camera. *(Writes)* "Available from Acme camera shop on Broadway."

JONI: I thought I put Press-On nails and a '50s skirt with a fuzzy poodle and chain . . . oh, here they are. While I'm at it, I should tell Dad about the pre-Christmas sale at Johnson's Hobby Shop. They've got Barbie 4-wheel drive Jeepsters on sale . . .

TONY *(looking through the lists)*: Did I remember to put a lighted yo-yo on my stocking list? *(Looks up and sees* JONI*)* Oh, hi, Joni. Whatcha doing?

JONI: Oh, I'm making out my Christmas gift list. You?

TONY: I'm doing the same thing. What're you giving your little sister?

JONI: Who?

TONY: Your little sister? You know, that little blond girl named Sara who lives at your house?

JONI: Oh sure, Sara. I don't know what I'm giving her.

TONY: I don't know what I'm giving mine, either. Boy, it's tough to pick out just the right gift for someone else.

JONI: Right you are, but that's what Christmas is all about, isn't it?

(Characters freeze for a count of three before exiting, or they may keep the freeze until the next song or scene is ready to start.)

Quick Tip This short scene is designed to get an audience thinking about what Christmas is and isn't. It does give the final answer. Make sure you follow it up with appropriate words and/or music that will deliver the real message of Christmas. If used in combination with music to bring the message home, consider the following transition:

Christmas isn't about *our* gifts, not the ones we want or the ones we give. Christmas is about *the* Gift, the Gift of all gifts. Christmas is about God's gift of Jesus.

Make Room for Jesus

A graded approach to the annual Christmas program using tableau and readers
by Debbie Salter Goodwin

Theme: Christmas

Uses: A Christmas presentation using all ages

Music: Add several musical numbers to make this a full-length program. Here are some suggestions: Begin with "O Come, All Ye Faithful," use "Rejoice" before Scene 7, use "You Are Lord to Me" Scene 9. Conclude with "When He Came."

Cast: 6 expressive late elementary READERS
Early and late elementary children to portray the following characters in 9 tableau scenes:
AUGUSTUS CAESAR
2 ROMAN SOLDIERS
MARY
JOSEPH
INNKEEPER
3 to 4 SHEPHERDS
3 or more ANGELS
3 to 5 SHOPPERS
2 to 4 welcome SIGN HOLDERS

Props: A black, 3-ring notebook for each reader
A large census scroll
*Swords for soldiers

*A sawhorse donkey for the Beth-
   lehem and stable scene
*Self-supporting sign that reads
   "To Bethlehem"
A manger with straw
A large cloth
*Cardboard cutout sheep for
   Scenes 5 and 6
A baby doll wrapped in cloths
Packages, shopping bags, Christ-
   mas lists, and a calendar for
   Scene 8
A banner sign that reads "Wel-
   come Jesus" for Scene 9

*Optional

Costumes: Biblical costumes to fit the
   characters in Scenes 1 through 7. Participants wear sandals or go barefoot.
   They may be as simple or as elaborate
   as you desire. Here are a few suggestions:
       A red cape fastened with a gold
          chain and buttons for Caesar
       Cutout poster board breastplates
          sprayed gold for soldiers
       White robes for angels
       Modern clothing for Scenes 8 and
          9

Stage: 6 standing microphones in the center of the platform are for the READERS.
   The scenes alternate on each side of

(Tableau) *Tableau* comes from the French word
meaning "living pictures." It is an ef-
fective way to use a few selected pictures to
tell a larger story. The easiest way to de-
scribe it to young actors is to call the scenes
"freeze pictures." In fact, you can play a
game of freeze in order to sculpt the scenes.
Give the actors plenty of verbal cues about
action in the scene, and ask them to pantomime (in place). When you see a picture
that works, call "freeze." Fine-tune as needed. Have the actors relax, and then ask
them to repeat the same picture without a
game of freeze.

   Divide the children into groups according to the scenes they will picture. In order
to give everybody a part, use different actors for each scene. If children are in more
than one scene, keep costume changes to a
minimum. A good way to get ideas for the
scenes is to look for pictures in Bible story
books or Sunday School papers. Compose
each scene to make sure that the audience
can see each face. Consider taking Polaroid
pictures to help the children remember
placement from rehearsal to rehearsal.

the READERS. If desired, erect large picture frames on each side where the freeze scenes will
take place.

Duplicate this page to give to the director(s) of the Tableau Scenes:

TABLEAU SCENES

SCENE 1: CAESAR'S CENSUS

CAST: Augustus Caesar and 2 Roman Soldiers
PROP: Census scroll

Caesar, with a scroll in one hand, gives an order to 2 Roman Soldiers standing at attention.

SCENE 2: TO BETHLEHEM

CAST: Mary and Joseph
PROPS: Sawhorse donkey
Sign: To Bethlehem

Mary and Joseph on the way to Bethlehem. Mary sits sidesaddle on a sawhorse donkey with Joseph pulling it. They both appear tired. Add a sign "To Bethlehem" if desired.

SCENE 3: NO ROOM

CAST: Mary, Joseph, and an Innkeeper

Mary and Joseph stand in front of an Innkeeper. Joseph is in a pose as if asking for something. The Innkeeper motions them to go away.

SCENE 4: AT THE STABLE

CAST: Mary and Joseph
PROPS: Manger
Large cloth

A manger and the sawhorse donkey identify the stable. Set the donkey as if eating from the manger. Let Joseph be spreading a cloth on the floor for Mary to lie down.

SCENE 5: SHEPHERDS SLEEPING

CAST: 3 to 4 Shepherds
PROPS: Cutout sheep

Shepherds are sitting on the floor, leaning against each other, sleeping. One or two cardboard cutout sheep are in place.

SCENE 6: ANGELS APPEAR

CAST: The same shepherds; add 3 angels

Angels join the Shepherd scene, as many as the picture frame will allow. The Shepherds change their positions to look at the Angels and register fear and surprise. One Angel to be the speaker in a central or elevated position.

SCENE 7: SHEPHERDS FIND JESUS

CAST: 3 to 4 Shepherds, Mary, and Joseph
PROPS: Manger and baby

Mary kneels by the manger tending a baby and Joseph stands nearby while Shepherds kneel near the manger.

SCENE 8: AT THE MALL

CAST: 3 to 5 actors
PROPS: Christmas packages
Shopping bags
Christmas lists
Calendar

Three to five actors picture a shopping frenzy. They are overloaded with packages, looking at long lists, checking their calendars, all with looks of panic on their faces.

SCENE 9: WELCOME, JESUS

CAST: 3 to 5 actors
PROPS: Banner sign: Welcome, Jesus!

Three to five children hold a sign that reads "Welcome, Jesus!" Add anything else to show how Jesus will be the central part of Christmas celebration.

(READERS *enter and stand in front of microphones. Tableau scene participants wait offstage in line in the* *order they will enter. While the* READERS *may need to pause for tableau scenes to get into place, practice to* *keep these pauses short and at a minimum.*)

R 1, 3, 5: The Christmas story . . .

R 2, 4, 6: . . . according to us!

R 1: It's a story that happened a long time ago.

R 4: How long ago?

R 3: I don't know. It happened so long ago it isn't even on my calendar.

R 5: Let's just tell the story.

R 1: It happened like this.

(*Scene 1 participants walk into place and take their pose.*)

R 1: You see, Augustus Caesar called for a census.

Scene 1

(*Stage right.* CAESAR *with a scroll in one hand, gives an order to* 2 ROMAN SOLDIERS *standing at attention.*)

R 2: What's a census?

R 3: It's a government thing. They make a law and then try to make sense of it or something.

R 1: It was a law that helped the government count everybody so they would know how much tax money they would get the next year.

R 4: It told them how many servants they could hire, you mean.

R 3: Anyway, that's how Mary and Joseph got to Bethlehem.

(*Actors for Scene 1 exit while Scene 2 actors take their places, stage left.* JOSEPH *brings the "donkey."* MARY *brings the "To Bethlehem" sign.*)

Scene 2

(*Stage left.* MARY *and* JOSEPH *on the way to Bethlehem.* MARY *sits sidesaddle on a sawhorse donkey with* JOSEPH *pulling it. They both appear tired.*)

R 5: It was a very long trip and wore both of them out, . . .

R 1: Especially Mary, because she was about to have a baby.

R 3: When they got to Bethlehem, they looked for a place to stay, but it was so crowded. . . .

R 6: You mean the Bethlehem Holidome had a no vacancy sign?

(*Scene 2 actors leave with sawhorse donkey, and Scene 3 actors take their places.*)

Scene 3

(*Stage right.* MARY *and* JOSEPH *stand in front of an* INNKEEPER. JOSEPH *is in a pose as if asking for some-thing. The* INNKEEPER *motions them to go away.*)

R 5: Nobody had a place for them to stay.

R 3: Not a single room.

R 2: Not even a back room?

R 3: Not even a back room.

R 4: Nothing?

R 1: Until somebody suggested the barn.

(Scene 3 actors leave and Scene 4 actors take their places. Mary *brings the manger with a cloth inside.* Joseph *brings the sawhorse donkey.)*

Scene 4

(Stage left. A manger and the sawhorse donkey identify the stable. Set the donkey as if eating from the manger. Joseph *kneels beside* Mary, *who sits, leaning against the manger.)*

R 2: With the animals?

R 1: With the animals.

R 4: Where did they sleep?

R 3: With the animals.

R 6: How did they put up with the noise?

R 2: Who cares about the noise? Think about the smell.

R 3: At least it wasn't crowded.

R 4: That's easy for you to say. Nobody asked the donkey.

R 5: While Mary and Joseph settled down for the night, there was another camp-out on a hill just outside of town.

(Scene 4 actors leave with manger, cloth, and sawhorse donkey. Scene 5 Shepherds *bring the cardboard cutout sheep and take their place.)*

Scene 5

(Stage right. Shepherds *are sitting on the floor, leaning against each other, sleeping. One or two cardboard cutout sheep are in place.)*

R 6: An all-night camp-out?

R 4: Sounds like fun!

R 2: I'm there!

R 1: But this was their job.

R 4: Sleeping?

R 3: No. Watching sheep.

R 6: How boring.

R 5: Well, it was about to get exciting.

(Scene 5 Shepherds *stay in place.* Angels *join the scene.)*

Scene 6

(Stage left. Angels *join the* Shepherd *scene. The* Shepherds *change their positions to look at the* Angels *and register fear and surprise. One* Angel *to be the speaker in a central or elevated position.)*

R 1: Suddenly the sky turned bright.

R 2: Like somebody turned on police lights or something.

R 3: And there were angels. A lot of them.

R 5: But they were there for a reason, and it wasn't to turn on the lights.

R 1: It was to make an announcement.

R 3: To deliver a message.

R 5: And this was the message:

R 1: A Baby has been born tonight—the Son of God.

R 3: And you can see Him if you go to Bethlehem.

R 5: You'll know you've found the right one if you find him wrapped in cloths and lying in a manger.

R 1: And that's exactly what they did.

(Scene 6 actors leave, and Scene 7 actors enter with the manger.)

Scene 7

(Stage right. MARY kneels by the manger tending a baby, and JOSEPH stands nearby while SHEPHERDS kneel near the manger.)

R 4: Did they find the Baby?

R 3: They certainly did.

R 6: How did they know where to look?

R 5: The angel told them.

R 2: So how many barns did they look in?

R 1: Nobody knows for sure

R 3: What we do know is that they didn't stop looking until they found Jesus.

R 5: Isn't that what Christmas is supposed to be about? Looking for Jesus?

(Scene 7 actors exit with manger, and Scene 8 SHOPPERS take their places with their props.)

Scene 8

(Stage left. Three to five actors picture a shopping frenzy. They are overloaded with packages, looking at long lists, checking their calendars, all with looks of panic on their faces.)

R 4: Is that why the mall is so crowded?

R 6: I don't think they're looking for Jesus at the mall.

R 1: Sometimes I don't think anybody is looking for Jesus at Christmas.

R 3: So why don't we act like angels and tell people where they can find Jesus?

R 2: I'm not searching in any smelly barn.

R 5: You don't have to.

R 1: Besides, the story of Christmas is that we don't have to look for Him anymore.

R 4: You mean like "Joy to the world, the Lord is come"?

R 3: That's right. Christmas means that Jesus came looking for us.

R 6: And too many times all He finds is a crowded mall and no parking place.

R 5: Worse than that. Our hearts are too crowded.

R 1: If you really want to celebrate Christmas, you have to make room for Jesus . . .

R 3: . . . in your heart.

(Scene 8 actors exit with props, and Scene 9 actors take their places with props.)

Scene 9

(Stage right. Two to four children hold a sign that reads Welcome, Jesus! Add anything else to show how Jesus will be the central part of Christmas celebration.)

R 2: Without Christ, all you have is a mess!

R 3: So here's the real story of Christmas.

R 4: God came looking for us.

R 5: He announced it loud and clear . . .

R 6: . . . with a baby.

R 1: He made himself easy to find . . .

R 2: . . . so that no one could miss Jesus.

R 3: So if you want to have the best Christmas ever . . .

R 4: . . . make sure Christ has the most important part.

R 5: That means to let Him have our heart.

R 1, 3 5: And that's the Christmas story . . .

R 2, 4, 5: . . . according to us!

(READERS *close their books, and everyone comes out to join* READERS *for a bow.*)

Rehearsal Help Don't neglect practicing with the readers by themselves. They need to be comfortable enough with their script to read with expression. They also need to rehearse with the scenes so they know how to time their narration in between and during scenes. Consider planting someone on the front row to cue READERS.

Plan a minimum of two group rehearsals. These rehearsals should occur *after* individual tableau scenes are ready and *after* READERS are comfortable reading the script together. Use the first all-group rehearsal to allow all participants to practice entrances and exits with props. Make sure everyone is in final costume for the second rehearsal. Practice with microphones at this rehearsal.

6
Kids and Music

One of the easiest ways to teach language to young children is with music. Is it any surprise that music helps teach children of all ages some of God's most life-changing truths? There's something about the melody and rhythm that echoes in the mind long after the CD or tape no longer plays. Music prolongs the life of a message. That's why this resource features the marriage between music and drama for kids: to prolong the message in the heart of the kids. Here are some ways to use music as a powerful tool in the lives of children.

- Use music to engage the child's imagination. What pictures does the song offer? What actions does the song emphasize?
- Use the song for its purpose first: worship, teaching, or celebration. Use it for performance second.
- Let the children experiment with ways to communicate the message of the song using props or movement.
- Introduce the song with a life-hook—a question or statement that intersects the lives of the children.
- Sometimes the music acts as an exclamation to the truth expressed in the drama. Sometimes the music takes the truth to a deeper level. Talk about the differences with the children.
- Consider ways to incorporate special performance music into the broader children's ministry. If it was worth working on for several rehearsals, it should be worth a more permanent place in children's worship and learning experiences.

♪ Music and Young Children

While music and young children are a good fit, there are some important principles to remember.

- Keep a structured rehearsal very brief. Attention span is rarely more than a minute per year of age.
- Use movement or rhythm instruments to hold their attention.
- Recognize that their physical and mental coordination is still developing. Some children will sing *or* clap. Involvement is the key.
- Make learning the music a game. Play *echo* by singing a phrase and asking the children to echo it.
- Incorporate the song into other activities. Use a praise song before prayer. Sing about the family, and then thank God for families. Let the song help the children express something to God.

Music and Elementary Children

Match the rehearsal method to the tone and rhythm of the song. Introduce quiet, reflective songs when you want the children to experience quiet. Introduce an upbeat song when the children need to move around.

Find ways to involve children who don't want to sing. Make them responsible for props.

Move them into drama-only parts. Help them find a way to feel secure and important. They'll be singing before the session is through.

Vary the way you introduce the music, rhythm, and words. Clap, stomp, or step out the beat. Hum or whistle the melody. Say the words together before singing them. Emphasize rhyme. Use it to help memorization. Use visual cues for words or phrases that are difficult to remember.

While it is always appropriate for the children to sing as a traditional choir, think of ways to group the children to allow movement that accents the words. Action underlines the words they sing. It helps communicate the message accurately to an audience and helps the children remember them as well.

Don't Forget

- Practice the transition between the end of a drama sketch and the beginning of the song. How will actors join the choir? What is the specific cue word or music?
- If the children will perform the song with action and movements, rehearse it regularly that way.
- Keep the message front and center. Encourage children to express the message with their faces and bodies.
- If different age-groups are rehearsing together, make sure to allow for different attention spans and learning levels.
- Many of the songs can stand alone without drama. Explore ways to add costumes and props and pantomime to a song.
- Find out how to incorporate a children's music special into a regular worship service. Just make sure the introduction and transition lead people to worship.
- Realize that there is rich overlap within the musical selections. Many songs have more than one use.

Time to Enjoy

Enjoy the way that music and drama make use of different skills and interests. Enjoy the expressions on the faces of children when the message hits home. Enjoy using music to share God's Word. With every musical note and rest sign, enjoy!

Songs for Your Programs

Bless the Lord

Words and Music by
JOANNE BARRETT
and RON LONG

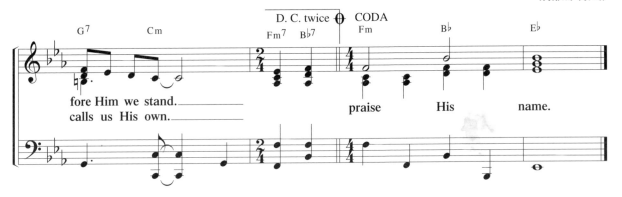

Clap Your Hands

Adapted from Psalm 47:1 by
GARY JOHNSON

GARY JOHNSON

Teach Me, Lord

LINDA REBUCK

TOM FETTKE

God Hears My Prayer

MILDRED SPEAKES EDWARDS

Old French Melody
*Arr. by Mildred Speakes Edwards
and Lyndell Leatherman*

Motions:
1. Point upward.
2. Cup hands behind ears.
3. Fold hands.
4. Motion outward.
5. Motion outward with other hand.
6. Point upward.
7. Cup hands behind ears.
8. Fold hands.
9. Cup hands behind ears.
10. Cross hands diagonally over chest.
11. Point to lips.

You Are Lord to Me

Words and Music by
TOM MCLAIN

You are my Lord; You give life to me.

You give me hope; You're my Prince of Peace.

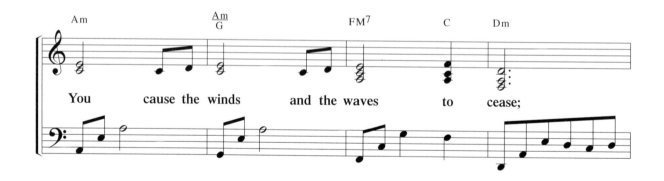

You cause the winds and the waves to cease;

You are___ Lord to me.

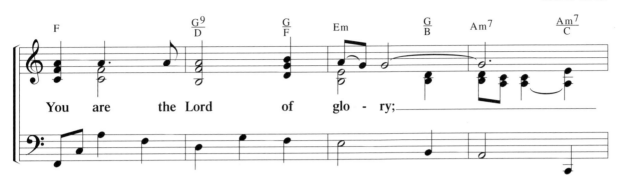

You are the Lord of glo - ry;

You are the Prince of Peace.

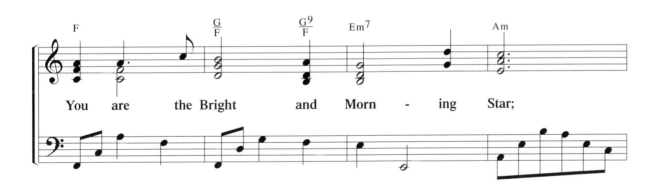

You are the Bright and Morn - ing Star;

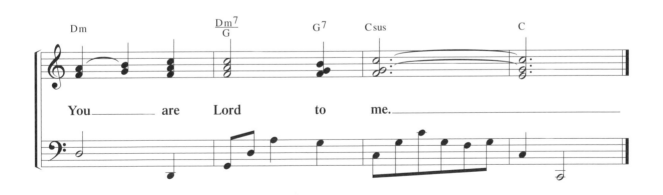

You are Lord to me.

I Will Trust the Lord

Words and Music by
STEVE SCHALCHLIN

I will thank the Lord in ev - 'ry - thing.

What a Mighty God We Serve

Unknown
Arr. by Lyndell Leatherman

What a might - y God we serve.

What a might - y God we serve.

An - gels bow be - fore Him; Heav'n and earth a - dore Him.

What a might - y God we serve.

He's Got Everything Under Control

Words and Music by
EDDIE SMITH

*Verses 1, 3-4 on recording.

felt those drops, he knew his God____ had ev - 'ry - thing un - der con - trol.____
God who____ made this u - ni - verse____ has ev - 'ry - thing un - der con - trol.____
God that al - lowed that fire to burn____ had ev - 'ry - thing un - der con - trol.____
God who____ made those li - ons growl____ had ev - 'ry - thing un - der con - trol.____

Refrain

He's got ev - 'ry - thing un - der con - trol;____ He's got ev - 'ry - thing un - der con - trol.

_____ The stars and the plan - ets are in His hand,____ The

wind and the rain at His com - mand.____ You and I, we're a

part of His plan.____ He's got ev - 'ry - thing un - der con - trol.____

Enough Love

LINDA REBUCK

TOM FETTKE

Noah

PAUL WILLIAMS
and DONNA WILLIAMS

PAUL WILLIAMS

1. No - ah, No - ah, Put the an - i - mals in the ark.
2. Rain came, rain came, But the an - i - mals all were safe.
3. Sun came, sun came, So the an - i - mals left the ark.

ark. They went in two by
safe. The wa - ter rose up
ark. They went out two by

two, Gi - raffe and kan - ga - roo. No - ah,
high; In - side the ark was dry. Rain came,
two, Gi - raffe and kan - ga - roo. Sun came,

No - ah, Put the an - i - mals in the ark.
rain came, But the an - i - mals all were safe.
sun came, So the an - i - mals left the ark.

Option: Create an "ark" by arranging chairs in the shape of a boat (with room in the middle).
Designate a "door," appoint a "Noah," and assign animal roles to the rest of the children.
Vs. 1: "Noah" leads "animals" into the "ark." Vs. 2: All stand inside the "ark." Vs. 3: "Noah" leads "animals" out of the "ark."

Jesus Loves

Anonymous

JILL FREEMAN
Arr. by Joseph Linn

Volunteers

Words and Music by
JOANNE BARRETT and RON E. LONG

Big Things

Words and Music by
CAROL GADDY
Arr. by Joseph Linn

We Are the Children

Words and Music by
TOM MCLAIN

and then He rose a- gain.
and He's called us to His light.

Jesus Loves the Little Ones

Traditional
Arr. by Lyndell Leatherman

1. Je-sus loves the lit-tle ones like me, me, me. Je-sus loves the
2. Je-sus loves the lit-tle ones like you, you, you. Je-sus loves the

lit-tle ones like me, me, me. Lit-tle ones like me
lit-tle ones like you, you, you. Lit-tle ones like you

sat up-on His knee. Je-sus loves the lit-tle ones like me, me, me.
saves them thro' and thro'; Je-sus loves the lit-tle ones like you, you, you.

We Are God's Children

Words and Music by
GRETCHEN KREIS

1. We've got a song____ to sing,
2. (*Whistle the melody or play it on kazoos.*)
3. As we go through____ each day,

we've got some news____ to bring, 'cause we are God's chil - dren.

we trust the Lord____ and pray, 'cause we are God's chil - dren.

Life is a joy,____ you see; We get our en - er - gy from

And if we ev - er fall We have a friend____ to call, 'cause

be-in' God's chil - dren.

we are God's chil - dren.

(1) In the morn-ing when we
(2) In the mid - dle of the
(3) Ev - 'ry eve - ning when the

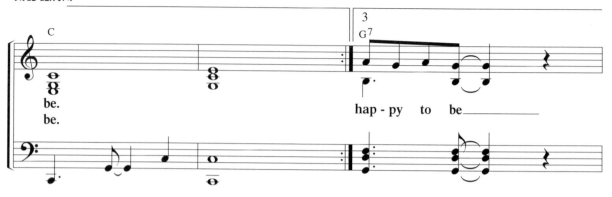

be.
be.
hap - py to be_____

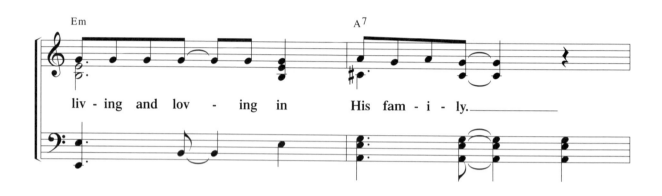

liv - ing and lov - ing in His fam - i - ly._____

We are God's chil - dren, and we got - ta keep sing - ing His

song._____

I'm Special

Words and Music by
LINDA WATSON

John 3:16

Adapted by DWIGHT UPHAUS

DWIGHT UPHAUS

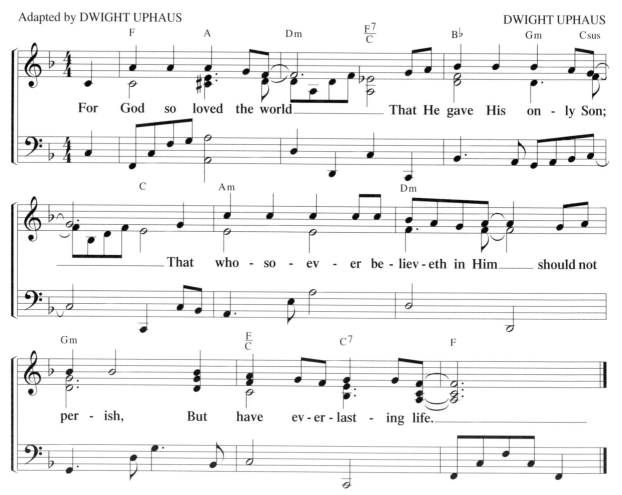

For God so loved the world_____ That He gave His on-ly Son; That who-so-ev-er be-liev-eth in Him____ should not per-ish, But have ev-er-last-ing life._____

Right Now

Words and Music by
OTIS SKILLINGS

Right now, right now, Com-mit your life_right now. De-

cide to live your life for Him right now, right now.

God Made Everything

Words and Music by
DORIS I. BLACK

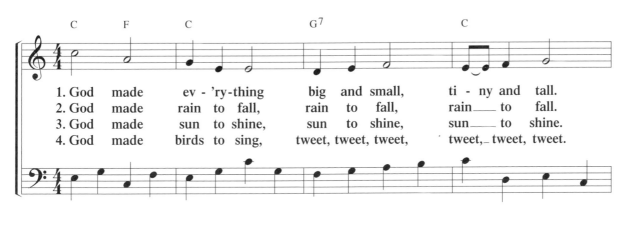

1. God made ev - 'ry-thing big and small, ti - ny and tall.
2. God made rain to fall, rain to fall, rain to fall.
3. God made sun to shine, sun to shine, sun to shine.
4. God made birds to sing, tweet, tweet, tweet, tweet, tweet, tweet.

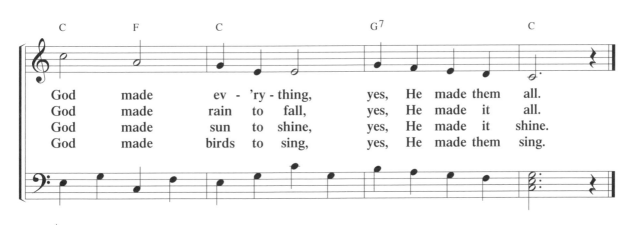

God made ev - 'ry - thing, yes, He made them all.
God made rain to fall, yes, He made it all.
God made sun to shine, yes, He made it shine.
God made birds to sing, yes, He made them sing.

Saints Society

Words and Music by
HARLAN MOORE
Arr. by Joseph Linn

Fast swing style ♩ = ca. 126

We're the Saints So-ci-e-ty,_____ Part of God's big

fam-i-ly;____ Kind and for-giv-ing, We're grow-ing and liv-ing in

Je-sus ev-er-y day._____ We're the Saints So-ci-e-ty,_____

Prais-ing God in un-i-ty;_____ Pray-ing and car-ing And

joy - ful - ly shar - ing His love for you and me. We're the

Saints So - ci - e - ty.

1. There is
2. Ev - ery

nev - er an - y ques - tion that we real - ly need each
one of us is spe - cial since we each have spe - cial

oth - er, For the Bi - ble al - ways men - tions "saints" as
gifts. God has giv - en us a way to help, to

sis - ters and as broth - ers. It on - ly takes just
care and love and lift. But e - ven though we

3rd time to Coda

107

two or   three_____   to make   a   "Saints   So   -   ci - e - ty"_____For
spe - cial - ize,_____   the hands   need   feet   and   feet need   eyes._____There's

Je - sus prom - ised   He would be   with   all   of   us to - geth   - er!
pow - er when we   re - al - ize   we   all   can work   to - geth   - er!

1st time: D.S.   CODA
2nd time: D.S. al Coda

We're the   al - ways vic - to   - ri - ous,

Giv - ing Him glo   - ri - ous,   Love and a - dor   - i - ous,   Tell - ing the sto   - ri - ous

Opt. div.

Saints   So   - ci   - e   - ty!_____

Just Say It

Words and Music by
MARTY PARKS
Arr. by Marty Parks

1. There are man-y ways to tell our moth-ers how we feel, And man-y ways to speak of our re-spect; But one that stands a-bove the oth-ers is i-deal, You'll nev-er find it in-cor-rect.

2. We can say it with our cra-yons and our fin-ger-paint, By be-ing nice when we would rath-er not; By do-ing all our chores with nev-er one com-plaint, But here's one way we like a lot:

110

Mom.   I love you Mom.

I love you, Mom."

A Happy Home

SUZANNE H. CLASON   Traditional

1. God told us how to have a hap-py home,   Have a hap-py
2. God said, "O - bey your par - ents in the Lord.   Do just as they
3. God said, "Be kind to oth - ers in your home,   Oth - ers in your

home,   have a hap-py home. God   told   us   how   to
say;   mind them ev - ery day."   God   said,   "O - bey   your
home,   oth - ers in your home."   God   said,   "Be   kind   to

have a hap - py home,   And____ live   for   Him   each   day.
par - ents and you'll have   A____ long   life   in   My   land."
oth - ers in your home,   And be hap - py ev - ery   day."

Lead the Way, Dad

Words and Music by
MARTY PARKS
Arr. by Marty Parks

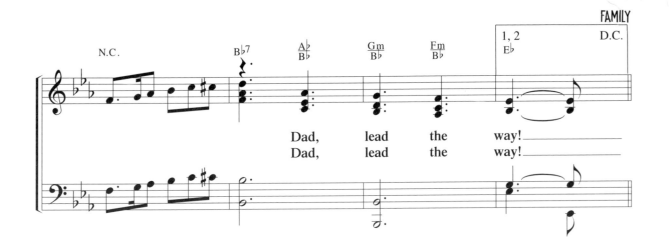

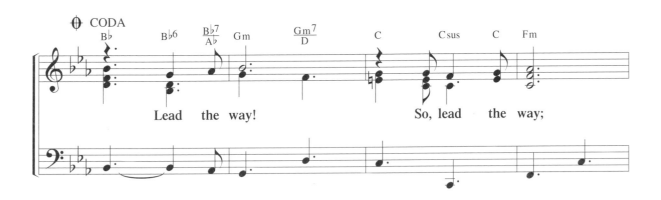

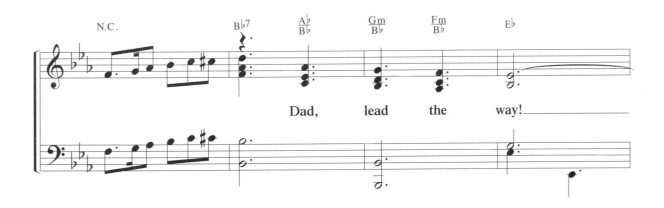

Easter Praise Parade

NAN ALLEN and
NANCY GORDON

DENNIS ALLEN
Arr. by Dennis Allen

He's Alive

The__ Lord is ris-en from__ the dead. The__ Lord is ris-en as__ He said. He's a-live! He's a-live! He's a-live!

Hosanna Song

Unknown

WILLIAM B. BRADBURY
Arr. by Lyndell Leatherman

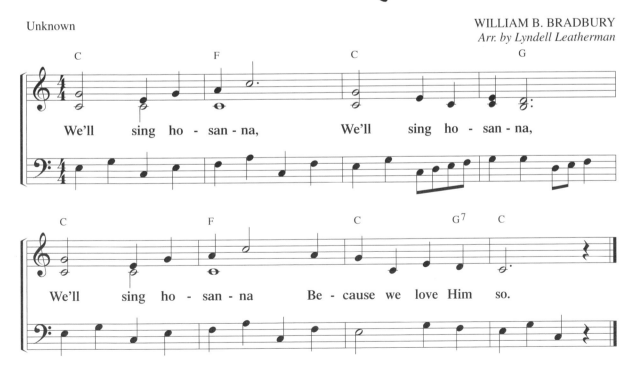

We'll sing ho-san-na, We'll sing ho-san-na, We'll sing ho-san-na Be-cause we love Him so.

Jesus Is Alive and Doin' Well

Words and Music by
EDDIE SMITH
Arr. by Joseph Linn

121

Here Comes the King

GORDON

DENNIS ALLEN
Arr. by Dennis Allen

Here comes the King,_____ here comes the Lord_____ of life!__

_____ Here comes the King,_____ here comes__ Je -

- sus Christ!_____ Here comes the King,_____

here comes the Lord_____ of life!_____ Here comes the King,_

O Come, Little Children

Traditional

O come, lit - tle chil - dren; O come, one and all! O come to the man - ger in Beth - le - hem's stall And see Ba - by Je - sus a - sleep on the hay. He came to bring joy to all chil - dren to - day.

Rejoice!

LINDA REBUCK
Gently ♩ = ca. 100

DAVID HUNTSINGER
Arr. by Joseph Linn

Shout for joy,_____ heav - en and__ earth. Cel - e - brate__ the Sav -

- ior's birth._____ · All of the earth and all of heav - en re -

joice,_____ sing and re - joice,

sing and re - joice!

127

When He Came

Words and Music by
MOSIE LISTER

O Come, All Ye Faithful

From the Latin, 18th Century
Tr. by Frederick Oakeley

From Wade's "Cantus Diversi," 18th Century
Arr. by Lyndell Leatherman

1. O come, all ye faith-ful, Joy-ful and tri-um-phant. O
2. Yea, Lord, we greet Thee, Born this hap-py morn-ing. O

come ye, O come___ ye to Beth - le - hem.
Je - sus, to Thee___ be all glo - ry giv'n:

Come and be-hold Him— Born the King of an - gels.
Word of the Fa - ther, Now in flesh ap - pear - ing.

O come, let us a - dore Him! O come, let us a - dore Him! O

come, let us a - dore Him,___ Christ___ the Lord!

Christ Was Born in Bethlehem

Adapted by EUNICE BOARDMAN

Early American Hymn
Arr. by Lyndell Leatherman

*1. Christ was born in Beth - le - hem, Christ was born in Beth - le - hem,
2. Mar - y was in Beth - le - hem, Mar - y was in Beth - le - hem,
3. Jo - seph was in Beth - le - hem, Jo - seph was in Beth - le - hem,
4. An - gels sang in Beth - le - hem, An - gels sang in Beth - le - hem,
5. Shep - herds came to Beth - le - hem, Shep - herds came to Beth - le - hem,

Christ was born in Beth - le - hem And in the man - ger lay. And
Mar - y was in Beth - le - hem Up - on that Christ - mas Day. Up -
Jo - seph was in Beth - le - hem Up - on that Christ - mas Day. Up -
An - gels sang in Beth - le - hem Up - on that Christ - mas Day. Up -
Shep - herds came to Beth - le - hem Up - on that Christ - mas Day. Up -

in the man - ger lay, And in the man - ger lay.
on that Christ - mas Day, Up - on that Christ - mas Day.
on that Christ - mas Day, Up - on that Christ - mas Day.
on that Christ - mas Day, Up - on that Christ - mas Day.
on that Christ - mas Day, Up - on that Christ - mas Day.

*Verses 1, 4, and 5 on recording.

Option: When they have learned the words, invite the class to dramatize the song. Choose one child to be Mary and one to be Joseph. The remainder of the class may be shepherds and angels. Encourage the children to plan their own simple actions to represent the Christmas story as they know it.

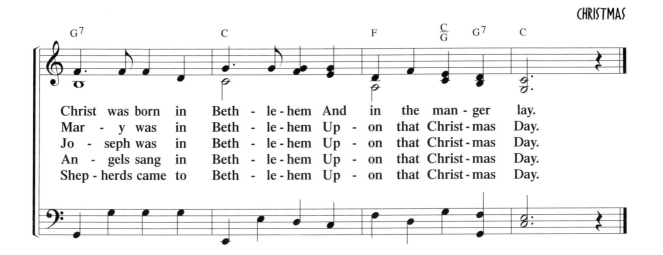

Christ was born in Beth - le - hem And in the man - ger lay.
Mar - y was in Beth - le - hem Up - on that Christ - mas Day.
Jo - seph was in Beth - le - hem Up - on that Christ - mas Day.
An - gels sang in Beth - le - hem Up - on that Christ - mas Day.
Shep - herds came to Beth - le - hem Up - on that Christ - mas Day.

Immanuel, Immanuel

Words and Music by
DAN WHITTEMORE

Im - man - u - el, Im - man - u - el, God is with us, Im - man - u -

el. They shall call Him Im - man - u - el, God is with us.

Im - man - u - God is with us.

131

Little Wooly Lamb

Words and Music by
NANCY HARRISON

Baby Jesus

Words and Music by
NATHAN CORBITT

Je-sus in a man-ger lay In a sta-ble low-ly.

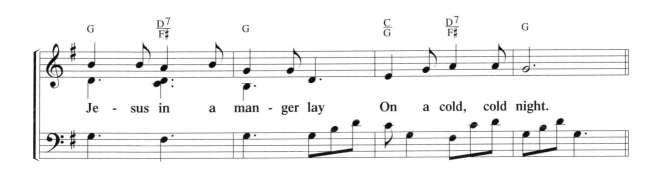

Je-sus in a man-ger lay On a cold, cold night.

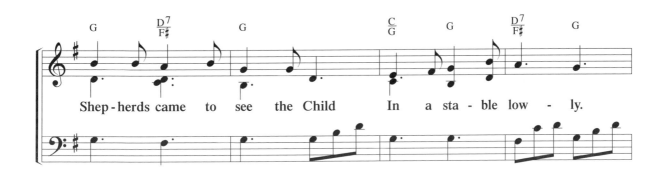

Shep-herds came to see the Child In a sta-ble low-ly.

Shep-herds came to see the Child On a cold, cold night.

Appendix

Programming Options

Think of your children's presentation as a carefully planned menu to celebrate a special day or focus on a special message. Use music, openers, two-liners, and longer sketches in a mix-and-match fashion. Sometimes a one-line transition gets you from one sketch to another. Other times, they follow each other without the need of transition.

Think about how to involve the whole children's division in a graded approach. Let the young children welcome the congregation and sing a song. Then, assign different sections to different age-groups. Use the age suggestions within the piece as it first appears in this book. End with a total children's choir number that summarizes the message you want to leave.

Here are some examples. Then, experiment on your own.

Raise Praise

("Raise Praise" becomes a continuity piece for this program about praising God. Use late elementary children to deliver "Raise Praise." Divide it as suggested. Use an adult or older child as the narrator to provide transition.)

Raise Praise 1

(Start at the beginning and take the piece through READER 4 *on page 17: Raise praise first.)*

NARRATOR: Three young men in Babylon learned how to praise God in a heated situation, and the people who saw what happened learned about God.

Three Men and a Fiery Furnace

"What a Mighty God We Serve" *(song)*

Raise Praise 2

(Repeat the first five lines then go to ALL *on page 17: Praise God for His all-knowing!)*

NARRATOR: God certainly knew a lot about a young girl and a whole nation's trouble. Everybody in this story had something to raise praise about. Everybody except one.

Esther

Raise Praise 3

(Repeat ALL *on page 17: Praise God for His all-knowing! Then go to end.)*

"Bless the Lord" *(song)*

Just Say I Will Obey

Welcome

Noah's Roll Call

"Teach Me, Lord" *(song)*

Three Men and a Furnace

"I Will Trust the Lord" *(song)*

RSVP

(A short scene between 3 boys acts as the glue to bring two sketches together. The theme is responding to God's invitation. Consider asking the pastor to make a closing invitation to everyone.)

BOY 1 *(holding an invitation):* I received this invitation in the mail, and it told me to be sure and RSVP. What does RSVP mean?

BOY 2: Ready, set, varooom! Pow! *(With appropriate sound effects and motions as if he's a racing car that crashes)*

BOY 3 *(shakes his head at* BOY 2*):* Maybe this will help.

Gates

BOY 3: Did that help you figure out RSVP?

BOY 1 *(scratching his head):* Not really.

BOY 2: What's wrong with ready, set, varooom, pow?

BOY 3 *(shaking his head at* BOY 2*):* Here's another scene that might help.

Too Much Money, Not Enough Heart

BOY 3: RSVP stands for some French words that mean, "please reply."

BOY 2: Like . . . make sure there's enough cake and ice cream for me?

BOY 3: Something like that.

BOY 1: I think I'm getting the picture. The invitation is only the beginning. In order to enjoy the party, I have to respond to the invitation. I have to RSVP. Which I'm going to do right now.

BOY 1 *(speaking to the audience):* The same is true with you.

BOY 2 *(speaking to the audience):* Jesus has invited you to RSVP.

BOY 3 *(speaking to the audience):* Isn't it about time you did?

"Right Now" *(song)*

God's Faithfulness

Esther

Shout for Joy

"What a Mighty God We Serve" *(song)*

For God So Loved the World
A missions presentation

Sketch: The Kingdom of Children
Song: "Jesus Loves"
Transition: God loved the world so much that He sent His Son. God also sent other messengers long before Jesus. Some of them weren't as anxious to go.
Sketch: The Jonah Rap
Song: "Volunteers"

A Presentation Idea Borrow the vaudevillian method of introducing each segment of a program with sign cards. Set up an easel to one side of the platform. Create colorful sign cards for each drama sketch and musical selection. Assigned children change the cards as participants get ready for the next piece.

His Kids
A Children's Day celebration

Here We Are

Growing

"I'm Special" *(song)*

Good Cooking

(Adapt the wording to cover the whole Christian education ministry. Example: change "teacher" to "teachers," "every child" to "all children," etc.)

"We Are the Children" *(song)*

A Heart for Jesus
A graded program for Children's Day or Mother's Day

From young children:
    Happy Hearts

From early elementary
    Gates

From late elementary
    The Parable of the Talents
    "Big Things" *(song)*
    "We Are the Children" *(song)*

The Gifts of Easter

(The three boys from Easter Gifts provide the continuity for this program. Note how the sketch is divided to insert music and story. Choose a stage position for the three boys that remains the same throughout the program. Practice ways for the boys to join the choir in the way that attracts the least attention.)

Welcome

Easter Gifts

(When DAN *opens the Bible, instead of reading John 3:16, have the choir sing "John 3:16.")*

"John 3:16" *(song)*

Easter Gifts, continued

(Replace BENJI*'s line "And He did that by giving up His Son to die." With the following:)*

BENJI: Maybe if we reviewed the last week of Jesus' life on earth, we'd understand. Do you remember how our _____ *(insert name of a children's worker or Sunday School teacher)* told the story last week?

Holy Week Live

(The choir members sit on the floor on one side of the stage so that they can give attention to the STORY-TELLER *who stands in the center. Story participants step out of the choir to take their places on the other side of the stage. At the end of Holy Week Live all move into three groups for the round, "He's Alive.")*

"He's Alive" *(song)*

Easter Gifts, continued

(Replace BENJI*'s line ". . . by giving up His Son to die" from page 45 with)*

CONNOR: Are you beginning to understand what the gifts of Easter are?

(Continue with DAN *to end.)*

"Jesus Is Alive and Doin' Well" *(song)*

Advent

First Sunday in Advent: Prepare

(Light the first candle of Advent.)

CHILD 1: The first candle of Advent represents God's call to prepare. Here is how some of us prepare for Christmas:

Christmas Lists

CHILD 2: Preparing for Christmas takes more than making a Christmas list. It involves getting your heart ready.

"O Come, All Ye Faithful" *(song)*

Second Sunday in Advent: Hope

(Light the second candle of Advent.)

CHILD: The second candle of Advent represents hope.

Praise the Lord

"Immanuel, Immanuel" *(song)*

Third Sunday in Advent: Love

(Light the third candle of Advent.)

CHILD: The third candle of Advent represents love.

Christmas Questions

"John 3:16" *(song)*

Fourth Sunday in Advent: Joy

(Light the fourth candle of Advent.)

CHILD: The fourth candle of Advent represents joy.

Jesus Joy

"When He Came" *(song)*

Warm-up Exercises

by Debbie Salter Goodwin

To get the creative juices flowing and encourage teamwork as well as work on a specific skill, consider how you might use the following warm-up exercises as you begin a rehearsal.

The Energy Ball

Purpose: To focus nervous energy and encourage teamwork.

A good exercise in the last few minutes before performance. Stand in a circle and instruct actors to put all the energy they feel into their fingers. They might wiggle them fast or even shake them. Start the energy ball by tapping someone on the back. That person must make eye contact and toss the ball. See how long you can keep it going.

Echo It

Purpose: To practice speaking loudly and clearly.

Divide the group in half. One half of the group waits in a line near the stage. The other half waits at the back of the auditorium. The group near the stage takes turns running to center stage and saying a line from a nursery rhyme like "Jack and Jill went up the hill to fetch a pail of water." If the group at the back hears it, they clap. If they do not, they yell, "We can't hear you," and the actor must repeat it. The rest of the stage group repeats the same line. At the end, the stage group and back row group switch places. ***Variations:*** *Choose a favorite line from the presentation to echo. Choose a line, and ask each person to repeat the line as a different character. Keep the same line, and use different emotions.*

Only Three Words

Purpose: To encourage facial and vocal expression and creative thinking.

Divide your actors into partners. Give each group three words to build a scene. They may not add any words, but they may repeat the words as many times as needed. Share each scene with the group as there is time, or bring a few back for each rehearsal.

Variations: *Allow the actors to polish their scenes, add a title, even simple costumes. Or let actors pick their own words and build other scenes. Or take some key words from your script, especially words you would like your actors to emphasize.*

A Helpful Reminder

Help kids remember their responsibilities by sending home this ready-to-copy reminder.

Remember

I promise to bring

_____

_____

for our next rehearsal on

_____

Questions?

Call

_____

Sketch and Music Grid

Section, Page	Sketch	Author	Age	Theme	Method	Music
Programs, 11	Welcome	Christine E. Scott	Young children	An introduction		
Programs, 11	Welcome Too	Martha Bolton	Early elementary	An introduction		
Programs, 12	Extra! Extra!	Amy Spence	Early-late elementary	An introduction		
Programs, 12	A Christmas Welcome	Brenda Wood	Early-late elementary	Christmas		
Programs, 13	Good Night	Christine E. Scott	Early-late elementary	A closing		
Worship, 15	Shout for Joy	Debbie Goodwin	Early-late elementary	Praise, God's greatness	Choral reading	Clap Your Hands
Worship, 16	Enter His Gates	Debbie Goodwin	Early-late elementary	Praise, Thanksgiving	Call to worship	Bless the Lord, Clap Your Hands
Worship, 17	Raise Praise	Debbie Goodwin	Late elementary	Praise	Call to worship	Bless the Lord
Worship, 18	Praise the Lord	Helen Kitchell Evans	Late elementary	Christmas, praise	Call to worship	Rejoice
Worship, 19	The Kingdom of Children	Kevin Stoltz	All	Missions, children	Choral reading	Jesus Loves, We Are the Children
Worship, 21	Here We Are	Faye Nyce	Early-late elementary	Children, missions	A responsive reading	We Are the Children
Bible Lesson, 23	The Creation Parade	Debbie Goodwin	Young children— early elementary	Creation	Rod puppets and Narrator	God Made Everything
Bible Lesson, 25	Noah's Roll Call	Martha Bolton	All	Noah, trusting and obeying God	2-actor sketch with optional pantomime	Teach Me, Lord; Noah
Bible Lesson, 28	Esther	Debbie Goodwin	Early-late elementary	Esther, God's faithfulness	Audience participation story	What a Mighty God We Serve
Bible Lesson, 30	Three Men and a Furnace	Kathy Ide	Late elementary	Daniel and his friends, God's protection, and faithfulness, obedience	Sketch with memorized lines, props, simple costumes	He's Got Everything Under Control (v. 3), What a Mighty God We Serve, I Will Trust the Lord
Bible Lesson, 33	The Jonah Rap	Judy Thompson	Late elementary	Jonah, listening to and obeying God	A rap	Volunteers
Bible Lesson, 34	Happy Hearts	Debbie Goodwin	Young children	The Beatitudes	Narrated story with props	Jesus Loves the Little Ones
Bible Lesson, 35	Gates	Debbie Goodwin	Early elementary	Discipleship	Narrator, pantomime, and simple lines	Big Things, Right Now
Bible Lesson, 37	The Unmerciful Servant	Jeffrey C. Smith	All	Forgiveness	An interactive story	Saints Society
Bible Lesson, 38	Parable of the Talents	Jeffrey C. Smith	Late elementary	Serving God	A narrated story with noisemakers	Volunteers, Big Things

Section, Page	Sketch	Author	Age	Theme	Method	Music
Bible Lesson, 40	Too Much Money, Not Enough Heart	Adapted by Debbie Goodwin	Late elementary	Discipleship	Readers theatre	Big Things, Right Now
Special Days						
Valentine's Day, 43	God's Love Gift	Martha Bolton	Late elementary	Love	Rhymed verse with props	John 3:16, Enough Love
Easter, 44	Something New	Debbie Goodwin	Early elementary	Easter, new life in Christ	An object lesson	He's Alive
Easter, 44	Easter Gifts	Paul Miller	Late elementary	Easter	A sketch with humor	John 3:16, Jesus Is Alive and Doin' Well
Easter, 46	Easter Joy	Tim Miller and Debbie Goodwin	Young children	Easter	Rhymed verse with simple costumes and props	Hosanna Song, Clap Your Hands, Jesus Loves the Little Ones
Easter, 47	The Praise Parade	Nancy Gordon, Dennis and Nan Allen	All	Palm Sunday	Sketch using music as the centerpiece	Easter Praise Parade, Here Comes the King
Easter, 48	Holy Week Live	Dave Tippett	Late elementary	Jesus' last week	An interactive story	Jesus Is Alive and Doin' Well, He's Alive
Mother's Day, 52	Sharing Love	Iris Gray Dowling	Young children	Mothers	Rhymed verse	A Happy Home
Mother's Day, 53	What Mother Means to Me	Iris Gray Dowling	Young children—early elementary	Mothers	Rhymed verse	A Happy Home
Mother's Day, 53	A Great Big Thank You	Rena Myers	Late elementary girls	Mothers	Rhymed verse with props and action	Just Say It
Mother's Day, 54	Doing Our Part	Margaret Primrose	Late elementary	Mothers	Rhymed verse with props and action	Just Say It
Mother's Day, 55	My Mother Is	Martha Bolton	Late elementary	Mothers	Rhymed verse with freezes	Just Say It
Promotion, 56	Moving On					
Promotion, 57	Growing	Debbie Goodwin	Young children	Promotion, growth	Short lines	I'm Special
Promotion, 57	Primary Spellers	Debbie Goodwin	Early elementary	Promotion, growth, Sunday School	Rhymed acrostic	Teach Me, Lord
Promotion, 58	Body Language	Debbie Goodwin	Middle elementary	Promotion, growth, Sunday School	A cheer	We Are God's Children
Promotion, 60	Good Cooking	Debbie Goodwin	Late elementary	Promotion, growth, Sunday School	An acted-out recipe	Saints Society
Father's Day, 61	Just Bragging About My Dad	Margaret Primrose	Late elementary	Fathers	Rhymed verse with props	Lead the Way, Dad
Father's Day, 62	F Is for Father	Wanda E. Brunstetter	Early-late elementary	Fathers	Rhymed acrostic	Lead the Way, Dad
Father's Day, 63	Short Subjects	Martha Bolton	Early-late elementary	Fathers	Humor	Lead the Way, Dad
Fourth of July, 64	God's Declaration of Our Dependence	Daisy Jenney Clay	Late elementary	The Bible in American history	Historical quotations	Teach Me, Lord

Section, Page	Sketch	Author	Age	Theme	Method	Music
Thanksgiving, 65	Thank You, God	Velda Blumhagen	Young children	Thanking God, prayer	Rhymed verse	God Hears My Prayer
Thanksgiving, 65	Our Thanks	Velda Blumhagen	Late elementary	Thanking God	Choral reading, call to worship	Bless the Lord
Christmas, 66	A Cradle	Mary Ann Green	Young children	Jesus' birth	2-line introduction to a song	Baby Jesus, Christ Was Born in Bethlehem
Christmas, 67	We Can	Mary Ann Green	Young children	Jesus' birth	2-line introduction to a song	O Come, Little Children
Christmas, 67	Jesus Joy	Robert Colbert	Young children	Jesus' birth	2-line introduction to a song	Baby Jesus
Christmas, 67	Christmas Questions	Paul Medford	Young children	Jesus' birth	Question and answer	Little Wooly Lamb
Christmas, 68	A Manger Bed	Wanda E. Brunstetter	Young children	Jesus' birth	Rhymed verse with props	Christ Was Born in Bethlehem
Christmas, 68	Happy Birthday	Paul Miller	Young children	Jesus' birth	A stanza to sing or recite	Immanuel, Immanuel
Christmas, 69	A Boy's Gift	Tim Miller	Early or late elementary	Christmas	Rhymed verse with costume	You Are Lord to Me
Christmas, 69	Christmas Lists	Paul Miller	Late elementary	Christmas giving	Sketch	When He Came, John 3:16
Christmas, 70	Make Room for Jesus	Debbie Goodwin	All ages	Christmas	Tableau and readers theatre	O Come, All Ye Faithful; Rejoice; You Are Lord to Me; When He Came
Other Programs						
Nonseasonal, 135	Raise Praise	Various	Late elementary	Praise	Readers theatre, a sketch, and a participation story	Bless the Lord
Nonseasonal, 135	Just Say I Will Obey	Various	Late elementary	Obedience	2 sketches	Teach Me Lord, I Will Trust the Lord
Nonseasonal, 136	RSVP	Various	Late elementary	Evangelism	Dialogue transitions with 2 narrated stories	Right Now
Nonseasonal, 136	God's Faithfulness	Various		God's faithfulness	Esther's story	What a Mighty God We Serve
Missions , 136	For God So Loved the World	Various	Late elementary	Children	Choral reading and rap	Jesus Loves, Volunteers
Children's Day, 137	His Kids	Various	All	Children are special	Short pieces for each age-group	I'm Special, We Are the Children
Children's Day or Mother's Day, 137	A Heart for Jesus	Various	All	Discipleship	Narrated stories	Big Things, We Are the Children
Easter, 137	The Gifts of Easter	Various	All	Easter	3 boys provide transition for music and a retelling of Easter week	John 3:16, He's Alive, Jesus Is Alive and Doin' Well
Advent, 138	Advent	Various	All	4 Sundays in Advent	Sketches	O Come, All Ye Faithful; Immanuel, Immanuel; John 3:16; When He Came

Music Index

Scripture Index

Index